CHASE YOUR DREAMS

JULIE ERTZ

HARVEST HOUSE PUBLISHERS
EUGENE, OREGON

Cover design by Kyler Dougherty

Front Cover Photos by John Todd / isiphotos.com ; USA Today

Front Cover image © Aerial3 / Getty Images

Interior design by Steve Kuhn

HARVEST KIDS is a trademark of The Hawkins Children's LLC. Harvest House Publishers, Inc., is the exclusive licensee of the trademark HARVEST KIDS.

Chase Your Dreams

Copyright © 2019 by Julie Ertz
Published by Harvest House Publishers
Eugene, Oregon 97408
www.harvesthousepublishers.com

ISBN 978-0-7369-7932-0 (pbk)
ISBN 978-0-7369-7933-7 (eBook)

Library of Congress Cataloging-in-Publication Data

Names: Ertz, Julie, 1992– author.
Title: Chase your dreams / Julie Ertz.
Description: Eugene, Oregon : Harvest House Publishers, 2019. | Audience: Age 8–12.
Identifiers: LCCN 2019007321 (print) | LCCN 2019008262 (ebook) | ISBN 9780736979337 (ebook) |
    ISBN 9780736979320 (pbk)
Subjects: LCSH: Ertz, Julie, 1992– Juvenile literature. | Women soccer players—United States—
    Biography—Juvenile literature. | Conduct of life—Juvenile literature. | Christian biography—
    United States—Juvenile literature.
Classification: LCC GV942.7.E77 (ebook) | LCC GV942.7.E77 A3 2019 (print) |
    DDC 796.3340922 [B]—dc23
LC record available at https://lccn.loc.gov/2019007321

Printed in the United States of America

19 20 21 22 23 24 25 26 27 / Bang / 10 9 8 7 6 5 4 3 2 1

CONTENTS

1

CHASING
A DREAM

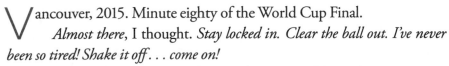

Vancouver, 2015. Minute eighty of the World Cup Final.

Almost there, I thought. *Stay locked in. Clear the ball out. I've never been so tired! Shake it off . . . come on!*

I looked around the field, trying to focus. I could see players warming up on the sidelines and talking to the coach. *Subs coming in*, I thought. *Stay on top of the changes.*

I couldn't remember ever being this tired. Surely the last ten minutes were almost gone . . . I glanced at the clock. *That was only ten seconds? You've got to be kidding me!*

The crowd had been roaring the whole game, but now, in the last minutes, they were in a frenzy.

Don't get distracted, I ordered myself. We went into a new formation. The faces of all my teammates reflected my exhaustion, but they kept shouting "Come on!" and "We've got this!" The clock kept counting down: three minutes, two minutes . . .

SO MANY SPORTS, SO LITTLE TIME

People ask me all the time, "Did you always know you wanted to be a professional soccer player?" The answer to that question is kind of tricky. It's not like I started playing soccer at four years old and knew right away exactly what I wanted to do with the rest of my life. In fact, I tried lots of sports before I fell in love with soccer. My dad was an athlete in high school and college, and he and my mom were big believers in the benefits of playing sports.

> We were always having so much fun outside that my parents didn't have to worry about our watching too much TV or complaining about being bored.

My older sister, Melanie, and I were always active. Our parents worked opposite schedules a lot, so when Mom was at work during the day, Dad would take us both out to the park or the playground—he says I could hang from the monkey bars when I was six months old. (With him ready to catch me, of course.) When my sister and I got a little older, our parents signed us up for sports. The nice thing about growing up in Arizona was that there was never really a time of year when we couldn't be outside playing: We swam in the summer, we played T-ball and softball, we tried basketball, and finally, we landed on soccer.

Trying all these sports at such a young age was awesome for a few reasons. First, we were always having so much fun outside that my parents didn't have to worry about our watching too much TV or complaining about being bored. It also gave us a chance to see what we liked and what we were good at. I found out pretty quickly that swimming wasn't really my thing—I preferred sports where the whole team was out there working together instead of each player working alone. Softball was too slow for me. I had too much energy to stand around waiting for the ball to come my way—I wanted to chase it! I liked basketball, but since neither of my parents was especially tall, I knew I probably wasn't going to have much luck in that department. So while none of these sports was an immediate hit, I was still learning a lot about what I liked and what I was good at.

Another nice thing about that time was that my dad was my coach during a lot of those early youth sports. My sister was shyer than I was, and "Coach Dad" helped her feel more comfortable in the field or on the court. For me, having my dad as my coach made it easy to be myself, and with him there to catch me (remember the monkey bars?), I wasn't afraid to try new things.

THE RIGHT FIT

When I finally started playing soccer, I loved it. It was fast paced and competitive, and I especially admired the teamwork part of it. It didn't hurt that my older sister (whom I followed everywhere) and a bunch of my friends played soccer too. I played my first full season with a recreational league when I was eight, and when the season ended, I couldn't wait for more.

When I found out that there was a nine-month gap between seasons, I knew I didn't want to wait that long. I'd tried enough other sports to know in my heart that I enjoyed soccer the most—and maybe that I was better at it than the rest of the things I had tried. My mom did some research and found a soccer club that had just started a developmental program for kids. It was based on teaching skills rather than on competing, and my mom thought that sounded perfect for my sister and me.

> I couldn't wait to get to practice at the end of the school day.

I absolutely loved it! The coaches were all PE teachers, so they were great at instructing and knew how to make all the drills and training really fun. I couldn't wait to get to practice at the end of the school day. On Saturdays, we would break up into teams and play each other, but since the program was all about learning, the competition came second to the skills we were practicing. Our parents were encouraged to cheer when we did a certain trick or used a skill we'd been working on instead of just when we scored points, and that really helped me fall in love with the game of soccer, not just with winning.

MOTIVATED AND INSPIRED

I don't remember being an especially great player at the beginning—I mean, how many people are just great at something right away? Not very many. When I watch old home movies of my early playing, I definitely don't think I was especially talented or any better than the average nine-year-old, but I was motivated and adventurous. My parents never pushed me or my sister more toward one sport than another, but when I decided I wanted to play soccer year-round, they helped me find a place to learn and grow. There's a lot more to tell about my youth soccer journey and all the steps I took to get to the Women's National Soccer Team, but that club is where my dream of becoming a professional soccer player first sparked to life.

> I don't think I was especially talented or any better than the average nine-year-old, but I was motivated and adventurous.

It's crazy to think about how much access girls today have to women's pro soccer. You can watch their games online, on TV, or in person if you live in a city with a National Women's Soccer League (NWSL) team, but when I was growing up (not that long ago), it was really hard to see women's soccer games. They weren't broadcast on TV, and you couldn't stream them on your phone. If I wanted to watch a women's game, I had to go in person, and the only women's team nearby was the Arizona State University (ASU) college team, so that's who I grew up watching.

ON THE FIELD

I was always excited when my parents would take me to see ASU play—those games were as close as I had ever gotten to watching professional soccer, and I wanted to be *just* like the players. I got to be the ball girl a few times, which meant I would hold extra balls on the sidelines during a game in case they were needed. I treasured every minute of it; getting to watch the game from right on the field was so cool, and I loved feeling like I had a part to play in the game, even a small one. I would sprint to give the team a ball when they needed it, and the excitement of sharing the field with those college players was huge.

We also got to have the girls sign our shirts when the game was over. I remember one player who had really blonde hair like mine and who was a midfielder like I was. I don't think I'd ever been so excited to meet and talk to someone in my life!

LEGENDS AND DREAMS

When I was about ten years old, right after the Olympics, the U.S. Women's National Team came through Arizona on their Glory Tour. It was the first time a women's pro team was going to be playing in Arizona, and our whole soccer team went to the game at Diamondback Stadium. It was the first time I watched women's pro soccer live, and it was the most exciting thing I'd ever seen. Mia Hamm, Shannon MacMillan, Brandi Chastain—those players are legends today because they did so much to put women's soccer in the spotlight, and to see them play live in the middle of their careers was *so* cool.

I remember watching these awesome women playing the sport I loved and thinking to myself, *Wow . . . that could be me someday!* Until that moment, even though I really loved soccer, I hadn't thought about it as something I could be when I grew up. But from then on, any time a teacher or a relative would ask me what my dream career was, I'd say "soccer player."

It's funny, because while playing soccer was the only thing I really wanted to do, I didn't start to seriously believe I could have a career as a pro soccer player until I got to college. Who cares what the opportunities or chances are when you're enjoying the game and enjoying the dream? I cheered until I was hoarse that day in Diamondback Stadium, and my teammates and I and thousands of other girls all went home imagining the day we would be playing for the Women's National Team. Did most of us make it? No, but does that mean it was a waste of a dream? No!

> The first time I watched women's pro soccer live, it was the most exciting thing I'd ever seen.

Over the next ten years, I would play hundreds of games and practice thousands of hours, and I knew there were no guarantees that I would play professionally. The thing is, the value of that dream wasn't in whether it was going to come true—it was in the hope and drive it gave me to persist through the tough times.

I still have the poster of the U.S. Women's National Team I got when I saw them on the Glory Tour. I remember that I wanted to get Brandi Chastain's autograph so badly. We waited with hundreds of other girls after the game, but we were too far down the line, and she stopped signing and had to leave long before she got to me. Brandi and I are actually really good friends now, and I've told her that story and we've laughed about it, but I still remember how bummed I was at the time.

Now when I'm signing autographs, I always think about that day, and I try to sign as long as possible for as many people as I can! It's so cool to think that one of those soccer-loving girls could be playing for the Women's National Team in ten years. So if you're ever waiting to meet me after a game and you don't make it, remember that you might end up on the team yourself someday, and you can tell me the story of how we almost met.

The dream gave me the hope and drive to persist through the tough times.

2

OUT OF YOUR COMFORT ZONE

What do you picture when you think of something that's comfortable? Your favorite pajamas? Maybe a really cushy couch or those reclining seats at the movie theater?

What about something that's uncomfortable? Now maybe you're thinking about new shoes that haven't been broken in yet, your desk at school, or holding your jaw open for a long time at the dentist.

Whatever you're thinking of, your definitions probably match mine. "Comfortable" tends to describe things that are familiar, easy, and safe, and "uncomfortable" is usually applied to new, strange, and difficult things. If someone asked you to pick between a pillow-top mattress and a concrete bench, it would be a pretty easy decision to go for the comfy option.

MY SAFE PLACE

The places you feel comfortable, the things you feel confident doing, and the people you feel the most at home around are sometimes called your "comfort zone." Everyone has one, and it's a good thing, because without those familiar, comfortable places and people, life would be way too stressful. The trouble is that by always playing it safe and staying where you're comfortable, you miss out on a lot of chances to grow and a lot of adventures.

> Most of my favorite experiences and biggest growth opportunities as a soccer player and a person happened when I stepped way outside of my comfort zone.

When I think about all of the most exciting, most amazing experiences I've had and the biggest opportunities I've been given, it turns out that almost none of them happened in my "comfort zone." In fact, most of my favorite experiences and biggest growth opportunities as a soccer player and a person happened when I stepped way outside of my comfort zone.

When I was growing up, my parents moved my sister and me around to several different elementary schools to make sure our schools and teachers were the best fit for our learning styles. I was often in the uncomfortable situation of being the new kid. At soccer club, it was different. I'd been with the same club since I was eight years old. I knew my coaches and my teammates, and if that wasn't enough, I was starting to feel like one of the best players on the team. It was my safe place, my "comfort zone," and I felt great there.

TIME FOR A CHANGE

I was twelve when my parents sat me down one evening to talk about my club.

"We've noticed you've been playing really well this year," my dad began.

Out of Your Comfort Zone 19

My mom nodded. "You've really been taking soccer seriously, and it shows."

"You've even talked about playing in college a couple times," said Dad. "Are you still thinking you might want to do that?"

I nodded. I *had* been starting to think about playing in college, but that still felt like it was a hundred years in the future.

"What's this about?" I asked. I was starting to feel nervous.

"Well, we think you need a different type of challenge from your current club," said Mom.

"You're a lot more serious and a lot more competitive this year, and if you're really passionate about wanting to get better and maybe play in college one day, we think it's time for a change," said Dad.

"You want me to change clubs?" I was in shock.

"I know it sounds scary, but I think you should consider it. A new setting and team with new challenges could really help you grow as a player," Mom told me.

Dad continued, "Do you honestly feel like you're being pushed to do your best where you are now?"

I was quiet as I thought about it. If I was being honest, the answer was no. I *didn't* feel like I was being pushed. Our training was good and we had a lot of fun, but most of the other players had a much more relaxed approach to the sport than I did—they enjoyed playing the game, but they had other interests

I knew that I wasn't going to improve if I didn't find a club that would challenge me, but I was dreading being the "new kid" yet again.

outside of soccer and different goals than I did. Even so, the thought of a new club, new teammates, and new coaches gave me butterflies in my stomach.

"We just think that this could be a great opportunity for you to try some new things and make some new friends," said Mom. The soccer player part of me agreed and knew that I wasn't going to improve if I didn't find a club that would challenge me, but I was dreading being the "new kid" yet again.

FINDING THE RIGHT TEAM

We decided that I would try out for three other teams in the area. I'm usually pretty outgoing and don't have a hard time making friends, but I remember how difficult it was to show up at those tryouts for teams full of strangers—I'd never been so nervous. I was worried about trying to perform for the coaches and show them my skills, but I also really wanted the players to like me.

My parents had been right—when I started comparing clubs, I quickly realized that if I was serious about wanting to play soccer, Sereno Soccer Club was the clear choice. My parents sat down with me again and let me know that this club switch would be a big commitment, but they would be with me every step of the way. And so we decided as a family that it was the right move.

THE RIGHT CHOICE

I spent the rest of my youth soccer career at that new club, and it was the best move I could have made for what I wanted to accomplish as a player. We won state every year, the coaches helped prepare me for college-level athletics, and my teammates became my best friends for the next eight years or more—I'm still in touch with a lot of them.

As part of that club, I was exposed to college showcase tournaments, I went to state and regional competitions every year until I graduated high school, and I played in front of lots of college coaches. All these amazing opportunities, and what was probably my biggest period of growth and improvement as a player, came because I moved out of my comfort zone.

Did I want to be uncomfortable at the time? No way! Was it scary to switch to a new club? Uh, yes! But if I'd stayed where I was, I would have stopped growing, and I would have missed out on so many awesome experiences and important relationships.

> If I'd stayed where I was, I would have stopped growing, and I would have missed out on so many awesome experiences and important relationships.

EXCITING ... OR TERRIFYING?

I'll admit, sometimes you don't see immediate results after trying something outside of your comfort zone. In fact, sometimes it's *so* uncomfortable that you still cringe remembering it years later. I remember one time after I'd switched clubs—I had made some great friends and was loving my new team—my coach told us about this really great soccer camp at Santa Clara University in California. It was going to be three days of skills workshops, games, activities, and guest coaches, and most exciting of all, Brandi Chastain was going to be there. I *had* to go. Even better, two of my best friends decided to go, and the camp was all we talked about for weeks—I feel sorry for our families.

Well, we made our plans, which included flying by ourselves out to California and back, something that we found insanely exciting and that made us feel extremely mature. But as (bad) luck would have it, a family conflict came up for one of my friends, and she had to back out of the trip. We were disappointed, of course, but my other friend and I were still excited—until another disaster struck and *she* ended up getting super sick.

Now suddenly I was facing not a fun adventure with my best friends but a trip to another state by myself for three days with a bunch of strangers. Flying alone wasn't exciting anymore—it was terrifying—and without my friends, I'd be assigned a stranger as a roommate. I wanted to back out too, but my mom had already paid for everything, so she strongly encouraged me to go ahead and go by myself.

> Brandi Chastain was going to be there. I *had* to go.

"It's only three days," she said, "and you were so excited! What about Brandi Chastain?"

"What about getting lost in the airport?" I argued, trying to keep the panic I felt out of my voice.

"We'll print off all the information you'll need about where to go once you land, and I'm sure the camp staff will be picking up lots of campers from the airport. You'll be fine," she assured me. (Though I'm not sure my mom was really less worried than I was; she called the camp directors three times to triple-check that someone was going to be picking me up from the airport and that they knew what time my flight got in.)

WHEN THINGS GO WRONG

So off I went to California, all by myself. I made it on and off the plane without anything going majorly wrong and arrived at the camp without any trouble. I was starting to be a little excited for all the soccer I was going to get to play and beginning to feel a little more hopeful that it wouldn't be completely awful. I was wrong.

The day before I left for camp, my cleats had broken, and with no time to replace them, my sister let me borrow hers. Now, my sister had been taller than I was for most of our lives up to this point, but I had just recently started to pass her by. I'd eventually end up being five inches taller than her and—I was about to find out—a shoe size or two larger. I hadn't tried the cleats on before I left, and when I put them on for the first practice session, I discovered they were a full size too small. I was miserable. Before the first training session was over, I'd gotten huge blisters on both feet that would only get worse as the camp went on.

That first night, the camp hosted a talent show, and that's where I finally thought I might start to enjoy myself, now that my poor feet could get a break. I met a lot of the other girls, but once the show started, I felt even more alone, as it felt like everyone had some amazing talent like singing or playing an instrument or dancing, and so I just sat there and watched, feeling more out of place than ever.

I had hoped I might make friends with my roommate, but she was even more homesick than I was and actually left the camp at night to stay with her mom in a nearby hotel, leaving me in our room alone. Feeling sorry for myself made me more homesick than I might have been otherwise, and I spent a lot of time staring at my one link with home—my mom's cell phone, which she'd let me bring in case of an emergency.

> I just sat there and watched, feeling more out of place than ever.

A BIG ACCOMPLISHMENT AND NEW CONFIDENCE

I was so unhappy the first night that I almost called to beg my mom to let me come home the next day. My blisters were so bad that I wasn't even enjoying the soccer part. Each day, the coaches would choose one player who'd been working especially hard or who had a really great attitude to be "Star of the Day." I wanted *so* badly to be chosen, but I could barely pass the ball because of the blisters, and my attitude certainly wasn't going to win any awards.

I did finally get to be in the same room as Brandi Chastain. I would like to say that hearing her talk to our group changed my whole attitude and the rest of the camp was amazing, but the truth is, though it *was* amazing that she was there, I still couldn't wait to go home—I was literally counting down the hours by the time the third day came!

> Having endured such an all-around uncomfortable experience gave me a lot of confidence going forward.

So what did I get out of that camp disaster? Well, for a long time I would have said "Nothing" and I would have meant it! It's still one of my most miserable memories. But does that mean I'm sorry I did it? Nope. (Not anymore, anyway.) So what if the best I can say about that camp is that "I survived"? Having endured such an all-around uncomfortable experience gave me a lot of confidence going forward. Was I happy to be back home where it was comfortable? Oh, yes—but knowing that I had been far from home, hurt, unhappy, and alone and had persevered was a really big accomplishment for me at that age.

TAKING RISKS

That boost of confidence was one of the best rewards for stepping out of my comfort zone. I remember at recess at school when I was younger, the older kids—mostly boys—would play soccer or kickball while the younger (and shyer) kids sat on the sidelines and watched. I knew nothing was stopping me from going over and joining the game. But instead, my friend and I would just sit there, wanting so badly to play but waiting for someone to ask us instead of just going for it. We were afraid we weren't good enough or that the older kids would reject us.

But after that miserable camp experience, you can bet that if I wanted to play soccer (and my shoes fit), I was going to play soccer, no matter who else might be playing first or what team I might have to share the field with. Taking a big risk made some of the smaller ones look much less scary.

> That boost of confidence was one of the best rewards for stepping out of my comfort zone.

Try to think about stepping out of your comfort zone as an exciting thing rather than a scary one. My professional career started because I took a big step into a totally new world. Growing up, my long-term goal was to play soccer in college. At that time, there wasn't a professional league for women in the U.S., so playing in college was my best chance to keep doing what I loved after high school.

The more I played at the college level, the surer I was that it was what I wanted to do professionally, but it looked like I was going to have to move overseas if I wanted to make soccer my profession.

NO BACKUP PLAN

At the end of my junior year in college, it was announced that a new women's national soccer league was forming. Suddenly, playing professional soccer in the U.S. seemed like a real possibility, but now I had a choice to make: Did I want to stay in the U.S. and be part of a brand-

> Try to think about stepping out of your comfort zone as an exciting thing rather than a scary one.

new league, or did I want to pursue a pro career in another country? Did I even want to try to play professionally with all the uncertainty that would involve? After playing for so many years in such well-established, familiar clubs and teams, the idea of fending for myself and taking my chances with a new or unknown team was pretty intimidating.

It was after I went to the U-20 Women's World Cup (an international championship for players aged twenty and under) that I realized, "Yes, without a doubt, *this is what I want to do!*" Something about playing in that international setting and with the best players my age affirmed what I had already known in my heart for a long time but had been afraid to make official—playing soccer was what I was meant to do, and I didn't want to do anything else or settle for any "backup plans." That's probably the first time I seriously considered chasing my dreams—I just knew how much I loved this game, and I wanted to follow whatever path would let me play as much as I could.

> Playing soccer was what I was meant to do, and I didn't want to do anything else or settle for any "backup plans."

"SEE WHAT HAPPENS!"

As the college draft for the new league's second year got closer, several other teammates and I started thinking very seriously about entering, even though it would mean leaving school if we were drafted. Playing for a pro sports team isn't like playing youth soccer, where you can just try out for whatever team or club you're interested in. The players were going to have to enter their names in a pool and then wait to see which team would pick them, if any. You might end up on the same team as your best friend in your hometown, you might end up two thousand miles away on a team full of strangers, or you might not get drafted at all. Talk about nerve-wracking. But my desire to play was a lot stronger than my fear of the unknown.

I talked with my parents and my then boyfriend (now my husband), Zach, and a bunch of the girls on my college team who were seniors as well, and they all said the same thing: "Put your name in! See what happens!" With no idea what the next step was going to be, I put my name in the draft and in January of my senior year got drafted third overall to the Chicago Red Stars.

> My desire to play was a lot stronger than my fear of the unknown.

Don't get me wrong—it was exciting to have been drafted and to have the chance to play professional soccer, but there were still a *lot* of unknowns ahead of me. This Southwest / West Coast girl knew nothing about the Midwest. I wasn't even sure where Chicago was! But when the draft was announced, I thought, *Well, I want to keep playing, and this is where that path is taking me, so here I go.* I didn't overthink it because I knew if I did, I'd get freaked out, so I took a deep breath and headed across the country.

"HERE WE GO—LEAD THE WAY!"

I showed up two weeks later than everybody else on the team because of my school schedule, so I was a little nervous at first. Everyone already knew each other, and here I was, once again the new girl. It would have been easy to give in to the anxiety and insecurity of being out of my comfort zone, but I'd been there before, and I knew that my biggest growth came when I pushed myself beyond what felt safe and easy. I still didn't know what this pro league adventure was going to look like, but I trusted that God had a plan and pretty much said to Him, "You know what? Okay, here we go—lead the way!"

Being out of my comfort zone also helped me realize how important it is to be kind to others who are in that situation. Having felt shy, alone, miserable, and out of place myself, it was easier for me to spot when others were feeling that way, and I hope it made me more ready to reach out and make them feel welcome.

> Being out of my comfort zone also helped me realize how important it is to be kind to others who are in that situation.

If you struggle with feeling confident in certain situations, or if you get butterflies at the thought of trying new things—whether it's trying out for a new team, auditioning for the school play, or going to camp—just remember that some of your most fun and exciting experiences might be waiting for you just a step or two outside your comfort zone.

3

IT'S ABOUT PEOPLE

Because both my sister and I played so much soccer when we were kids, people assume our family must have been "all about soccer." Sure, we spent a *lot* of time driving to and from practice in my mom's maroon van (nicknamed "The Cranberry"), and most of our family trips were organized around tournaments and championship games, but if I had to pick one thing my family was "all about" when I was growing up, it would be people.

My parents lived by the Golden Rule: Do unto others as you would have them do unto you; treat people how you want to be treated. My parents showed consideration for others in the smallest ways, like holding the door open for someone or saying thank you. They showed my sister and me that these seemingly little acts were actually important messages to people, like saying "I see you" and "I genuinely appreciate you." My parents taught us how blessed we were to have the opportunities we did and how vital it was to give back and serve others as a way of showing our gratitude.

"HOW CAN I HELP?"

"How can I help?" are four really simple words, but my mom showed me what a big different asking that question and really listening to the answer can make in a person's life. At our soccer club, at our church, or in our neighborhood, I heard Mom ask people over and over, "How can I help?" My mom's a nurse, so the desire to help people has always been a big part of who she is. Nurses have demanding jobs with long hours, so many people felt that my mom would have been justified in taking some time for herself when she wasn't working, but what I remember is that Mom used most of her time off doing things for other people.

> There was no such thing as "too busy" to help or "too important" to serve.

If the church or soccer club needed to hold a bake sale or a car wash to raise money, my mom would jump right in and make it happen. But what I remember even more are the small ways my mom served others and made them feel important. If a new neighbor moved into the cul-de-sac, Mom would have us all go over and introduce ourselves (usually with a batch of cookies). If someone she knew was having a birthday, she tried to make it special. She made sure to thank our teachers with little gifts on holidays and at the end of the school year. She went the extra mile to let people know they were appreciated.

Mom's "How can I help?" motto was contagious! My parents made sure we knew there was no such thing as "too busy" to help or "too important" to serve. With their kids' crazy soccer schedules and their work, it would have been easy for my parents to say "It's important to serve when you have time" or "It's important to give back out of your extra," but there were no disclaimers on loving other people and no excuses for not doing it.

SERVING BY PAYING ATTENTION

Serving others to give back took on a whole new meaning when I got to college. Leaving my home and club behind really changed my perspective. I'd been in that kind of family environment for so long, it had been a while since I'd gotten to see the amazing way sports can bring together people from different places, backgrounds, and experience levels. Now I was meeting girls from all over the country who had the same goal as me, and even though most of us had never played together, we all loved the same game. Not only that, but I was meeting young players from the community around the college and even getting the chance to coach them.

One of my mentors in college was a wonderful, caring Santa Clara alum named Michelle, who introduced me to her equally wonderful best friend, Jodi, who coached her own club in the area. The players from Jodi's club would visit the campus to watch a game. I remembered how cool I'd thought it was to see the Arizona State University (ASU) women's team play when I was their age, and I tried to give the girls some extra attention, learning their names and giving them a smile or a high five when I saw them—the kind of thing that would have meant so much to me as a young player.

THE JOY OF COACHING

After a month or so, Jodi asked a few of my teammates and me if we wanted to help out with coaching in our spare time. I wasn't sure at first. I was captain of the Santa Clara team, but coaching younger girls felt a little intimidating. Sure, I could play, but could I teach? Would they listen to me? But I loved the idea of spending more time with Jodi and Michelle, and I wanted to invest in those girls' lives the way older players had invested in mine. Even more than that, I wanted to help them love the game as much as I did, so I cautiously said yes.

> I wanted to invest in those girls' lives the way older players had invested in mine.

I absolutely loved it! At that point in my life, having just made the transition from youth soccer to a college team and starting to dream about a professional career, it was so cool for me to be out there watching the next generation of players. I recognized the girls' excitement and joy as the same excitement and joy I had when I was their age, and it really showed me just how far I'd come.

As part of my involvement with the team, I worked one-on-one with some of the players, teaching specific skills or building confidence, and it was so gratifying when a girl I'd coached came back the next week and told me about how she'd used what we'd worked on or finally conquered a tricky move during a game. It made me understand why so many people love the undeniably tough job of teaching, because seeing the delight on a player's face when her hard work and training translated to success on the field was one of the most rewarding experiences I've ever had.

GIVING AND RECEIVING

I firmly believe that you get back more than you give when you give of your time and of yourself. One of the things that surprised me the most about my coaching experience was how much *fun* I had! I went into it expecting to provide a service, to volunteer and hopefully make a difference, but I kind of expected it to feel like a chore or a duty. I did not expect to jump up and down with excitement when a young player told me about scoring a goal or to smile so much watching those girls play and improve.

Coaching also taught me a lot about what it really means to give of yourself. These girls didn't need money or equipment or opportunities from me—they needed my time and attention. They also needed me to have qualities that I sometimes had to work to bring out! For instance, I learned a lot

> Seeing the delight on a player's face when her hard work and training translated to success on the field was one of the most rewarding experiences I've ever had.

about patience as a coach. One thing I love about kids is that they're always asking questions and always want to know the "why" behind what they're doing. I discovered quickly that "Because that's just how it is" is not an answer that satisfies them! Coaching really made me think about the reasons behind doing something a certain way and forced me to communicate clearly when a player was having trouble instead of just getting impatient with her. Teaching those girls left me with a new appreciation for my own coaches and the time and effort they put into teaching me!

A BIGGER EFFECT

I also realized I had the potential to influence others—for better or for worse. Suddenly I was in a position where young girls were looking up to me like I had looked up to the ASU players just a few years before. I started to comprehend then that I didn't want to be *just* a soccer player. I didn't want my identity to be tied up in that one thing. I loved that those girls loved to watch me play, but I wondered, *If my main value is in being good at soccer,*

> I wanted to be more than a player who was fun to watch; I wanted to give back to people who looked up to me in a meaningful way.

what reason do these girls have to look up to me when I'm not playing well? What if I had a bad game or a rough season?

I wanted to be more than a player who was fun to watch; I wanted to give back to people who looked up to me in a meaningful way. But how could I do that? The question stuck with me throughout college and into my professional career. Just like my mom, I found myself asking more and more, "How can I help?"

WHERE TO START?

After I'd been playing professionally for a couple of years, I started to pay more attention to how other people were answering that question. At my Bible study in Philly one night, we were talking about what it looks like to serve others. A friend told the story of how she had been outside with her young daughter on a freezing-cold day when a woman came hurrying by, carrying a baby with no coat on. My quick-thinking friend, who was only half a block from home, took off her daughter's jacket and gave it to this woman's baby—a simple gesture but a powerful act of kindness. I wanted to give people that kind of tangible help, but where was I supposed to start? There were needs everywhere—how was I supposed to meet them all or even decide which ones to meet?

At the same time, I was surrounded by people who were giving back on a huge scale through foundations and charities they had either started or worked very closely with. A foundation is a nonprofit organization, which means it doesn't exist to make money. Some foundations exist to help a specific cause, while others give money and support to several different groups.

AN INSPIRING VISION

Many professional athletes who want to help people who are less privileged than they are start foundations. When my husband, Zach, and I started attending events hosted by these nonprofit foundations, we loved learning about how the organizers were touching lives. Giving money through a foundation might not be as personal as giving someone a coat on a cold day, but Zach and I were just as inspired, and we started to grow a vision of starting our own foundation one day.

In 2018, Zach had the incredible opportunity to travel to Haiti on a mission trip with some of his teammates. I had a tournament, so I wasn't able to go, but I vividly remember the phone conversation we had after he had been there a few days.

> I wanted to give people that kind of tangible help, but where was I supposed to start?

"How's it going?" I asked eagerly.

"Good!" Zach said. "We've just been helping out with some work projects, sharing the Word where we can, getting to know the people—stuff like that." Zach's voice was excited. "The people are amazing! They have so little, but they have so much hope and joy in life . . . it's unbelievable!"

He told me about several of the people he'd met—they had lost loved ones in the hurricane, they were homeless or sick, but they were so full of love and compassion for each other.

"I played soccer with some kids today!" he said.

"Really? That's awesome!"

"Yeah! They just had one old soccer ball, and the field was full of holes, but they were having a blast. We all were! They were just so happy to be playing and to have us there with them. A couple of them were kicking around a water bottle full of dirt on the sides because there was only one ball, but they were having so much fun. You would have loved to see it."

"LET'S GO FOR IT!"

I thought about that story long after Zach and I hung up. I loved that those kids were finding a way to enjoy soccer despite the circumstances, but I was also humbled by how privileged my own childhood had been.

> I wanted to give as many kids as possible access to the same joy and strength of character I had found in playing soccer.

I thought of the perfect green fields of my club growing up and the endless supply of uniforms and cleats my parents had supplied, and I wondered if I would have still been able to find joy in the game without those things.

I knew then I wanted to do more to give as many kids as possible access to the same joy and strength of character I had found in playing soccer. Zach and I knew we wanted to give back to our communities, and we knew a foundation was the best way to help the most people in the long term. The trip to Haiti was the tipping point for Zach. When he came back, he said, "It's time. Let's go for it." The need he had seen had moved us both to start helping on a larger scale. We knew we couldn't solve every problem or help every person, but it was time to ask, "How can we help?"

THE ERTZ FAMILY FOUNDATION

This time, we answered that question by creating the Ertz Family Foundation. Our nonprofit creates sports and education opportunities for kids who don't have the resources we had. Coaching in college let me see firsthand how much fun kids can have and how much they grow when they play sports, and I've never lost my passion for giving kids that opportunity.

I think young players have a special place in my heart because I also
get excited at any chance I have to
learn. Young players are constantly
learning—about the game, about their
strengths and weaknesses, about teamwork, about who they are and who they
want to be—and I strongly believe that
playing sports, especially a sport like soccer, is a privilege kids will benefit from
for the rest of their lives.

> Young players have
> a special place in my
> heart because I also
> get excited at any
> chance I have to learn.

CREATING OPPORTUNITIES

Another goal of our foundation is to help get kids excited about education at every level. After we started our nonprofit, one of the first things
we did was create a college scholarship fund specifically for students from
Haiti. Since our whole foundation was kicked off by Zach's trip, we wanted
to start by creating opportunities that otherwise would have been out of
reach for students in a country facing such massive challenges.

In the Bay Area, where Zach is from, our foundation created a tutoring
service for some of the soccer and foot-
ball teams to help the players study for
the SATs. In Philly, where Zach's football
team is based, we heard about a youth
football team that got all their equipment
stolen and couldn't afford to replace it.
They were going to have to forfeit their

> Knowing how blessed
> we've been, doing
> nothing is just
> not an option.

football season, but our foundation was able to help raise funds to get them new equipment. These are still comparatively tiny services, but in the face of all the need out there—and knowing how blessed we've both been in our lives—doing nothing is just not an option.

TIME AND ATTENTION

Maybe you're hearing all this and thinking, *Well sure, when I'm an adult and a pro athlete, then I'd love to help people out that way, but what can I do now?* One of the biggest ways you can make a difference in people's lives right now is with your time and attention. Take the time to be kind to someone, work with a teammate on something she's struggling with, or help a friend who's having a hard time in school. Even simpler, just listen to people!

> One of the biggest ways you can make a difference in people's lives right now is with your time and attention.

My friend's son is the most outgoing, engaging person I've ever met. Talking to him makes me feel great because he's full of questions about my life and seems genuinely interested in the answers. Anybody can have hundreds of "friends" on Instagram or Snapchat, but when hard things happen in your life, those relationships aren't going to be much of a substitute for real friendships with people who really care about you. Making real connections by truly listening to others is how you cultivate the kinds of friendships that make the world a more caring place.

THE BEST KIND OF HELP

I guess the biggest thing I've learned about giving back is that the most important part of serving others is not the size of the service or the price of the gift but your heart for the people you're helping. When you ask "How can I help?" you're not just asking what you can do for others—you're asking, "What do they need? What are their problems? What's going on in their lives?"

It's easy to disengage from people and have superficial interactions through a cell phone. It's easy to disconnect from people around us and spend our time "connecting" online—but that kind of connection isn't real, and it leaves everyone feeling lonely.

> I love really learning about another person's story and her situation.

I love really learning about another person's story and her situation. Too often we miss out on opportunities to really get to know someone because we're on our phone or wrapped up in our own thoughts and worries, and by the time we look up, that chance to connect with and care about someone else is gone.

START SMALL

If you want to change the world, I've come to agree with my parents that it really does start with small things that make other people feel truly seen, like holding a door open or taking a moment to listen after asking "How are you?" So engage with people, say hi! Don't settle for robotic "How-are-you-I'm-fine" conversations. Try leaving your phone in your pocket once in a while!

I try to be as present and undistracted as possible when I'm meeting fans or when I talk to my friends because I want to send the message that people are worth my time and attention. Making the extra effort to serve others is good for you and others. It's so easy to get caught up thinking about yourself, but really listening to and caring about others gets you out of your own head and makes your own problems seem smaller every time.

4

FAITH

Has a teacher or a friend ever asked you to describe yourself in three words? The idea is that you pick three words that best represent who you are, whether that's your hobbies, the people you love, or a quality you possess. You might pick "skiing, kind, ice skating" or "loyal, violin, brave." For a lot of my life, my words would have been "soccer, soccer, soccer." The words you choose say a lot about your identity, or your sense of who you are and what defines you.

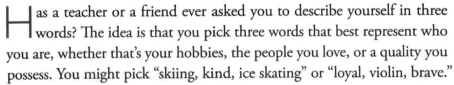

What I *do* is play soccer, but who I *am* is a question I struggled to answer for years.

My identity has been tied to soccer for almost as long as I can remember. Growing up, everybody at school knew I played soccer because I was always missing birthday parties and school dances to go to practice or a game. In college, I was immediately "one of the soccer players" on campus, and that's how everybody knew me. Now that I play professionally, that's how most of the world knows me: "Julie Ertz, soccer player."

Now obviously, I *love* soccer, and I love that I get to play professionally. I'm still in awe that so many young players look up to me and want to be like me, but I've learned there's a difference between what you *do* and who you *are*. What I do is play soccer, but who I am is a question I struggled to answer for years.

MY FAMILY'S VALUES

I grew up going to church with my family. In church, my sister and I learned we should be kind, humble, and loving, and that's exactly how our parents raised us, so going to church always felt normal. I believed in God and Jesus, and I accepted the lessons I learned at church because they were the same lessons my parents worked to instill in me—caring for others, telling the truth, not stealing or being disrespectful. I didn't really understand what having a relationship with God meant. I believed what He said in the Bible, and I thought that was all there was to it. I always heard "God is love" and "God is always there for you," which made Him a comforting presence in my life, but I didn't quite grasp that there was more to having a relationship with Him than that.

A DIFFERENT APPROACH

In middle school, I noticed my best friend, Sarah, had a different approach to God and church. Jesus was a real person in her life—someone who loved her and was always there for her—and I saw how that made a difference in how she approached life. Sarah and I and our teammates hung out at Sarah's house a lot in middle and high school. Sarah's mom, Delayne, was like another mom to all of us, and as we went through the usual struggles and challenges of growing up, Delayne constantly set the example of leaning on her faith and encouraging Sarah to do the same.

Another of my really good friends, Ellen, was in a similar place with her faith—she never claimed to have all the answers, but she knew she was doing life with God alongside her and was always willing to take her questions to Him.

> They had the hope and assurance that God was a real presence in their lives, someone who was there for them and could be trusted no matter what.

I think what appealed to me most about these friends' approach to faith was that they never pretended they had everything figured out, and they never acted as if having a relationship with God made them perfect. Rather, they had the hope and assurance that God was a real presence in their lives, someone who was there for them and could be trusted no matter what. Their relationships with God were authentic and unconditional, even when they made mistakes or bad choices. They showed me that faith is a journey, a process, rather than something you find or achieve all at once. Seeing what my friends' relationships with Jesus looked like helped me start to understand that faith journey and to take steps toward experiencing a similar relationship myself.

There are moments in life when you might find yourself questioning where your value comes from. You might even feel like your worth is tied to what you do—how good a soccer player you are, how good a student you are, how many friends you have. My parents were wonderful and very supportive whenever I was going through something hard, and my friends and teammates always tried to be encouraging and positive, but at that point in my life, I realized none of the things I used to measure my worth were lasting.

My sophomore year, I had an injury that I thought might put an end to my dreams of playing soccer in college. I didn't realize until I was facing that possibility just how much I relied on soccer for my sense of worth. Injuries happen, friendships change, grades slip, you grow up and leave your family, and sometimes you lose the soccer game, so if I wanted lasting security—the kind that comes from having someone in your life who never leaves, never changes, and loves you unconditionally—I needed a closer relationship with Jesus.

> I didn't realize just how much I relied on soccer for my sense of worth.

Sarah and Ellen showed me what it looked like to have a personal relationship with Jesus, to have Him as a constant presence in my life. They helped me learn just how much He loved me—not because I was a really good soccer player or a good person or great student but because I was Julie, His creation and His daughter. It would be several years before I really learned that lesson fully, but lucky for me, Jesus is very patient!

A CRISIS OF FAITH

I had what you might call a "crisis of faith" in college. You might have heard someone use that phrase before—it just means reaching a point in your life when you have to decide if you really believe what you say you do, and if so, you have to live differently because of it. You can float along vaguely believing Jesus died for you, but if you don't decide to act on that belief and accept that sacrifice, your "faith" isn't going to help you much when life gets tough.

When I first got to college, I had to deal with a lot of change. Away from home and my family, away from my old club and everything familiar, I was playing with new teammates and for new coaches and living in a different state, and I just felt *lost*. College is a time when you really start to pay attention to who you are and who you're becoming—when you start to settle into your identity or make strides toward a new one. But I wasn't satisfied with any of what I was learning about myself.

I still loved soccer, but I didn't know who I was when I wasn't playing. The last five or six years of my life had led up to this moment, and now here I was, asking myself, "So what? Now what?" I found myself looking for my purpose in life, wondering what I was there for. On the field, I still had the old drive to succeed and to chase my goals. Off the field, I felt like I needed more in my life, but I didn't know what or where to find it.

Being "Julie the soccer player" was all I'd been trying to be for so long, but now that I was living my dream, it felt flat somehow. I didn't know my purpose or even my value apart from what I did on the soccer field, so I started trying to find it in other places and through other things. I didn't quite go crazy, but I wasn't making the best choices, and all the time I was ignoring the root of the problem. It wasn't an issue with the school or the team or even with soccer—my heart just wasn't in the right place.

> I still loved soccer, but I didn't know who I was when I wasn't playing.

FINDING MY PLACE

An amazing man named Sherman volunteered for our team. Sherman knew a lot of us were far away from home, and he and his wife worked hard to make us feel welcome and cared for. They invited the team to their weekly Bible study. Every week, Sherman's wonderful wife would make us dinner (a great way to show college students you love them is to feed them), and they both would run the Bible study.

My best friend, Sarah—yes, the same one from middle school—had ended up at the same college, and she and another friend of ours were really

> I'd gotten closer to Jesus in high school, but I felt so disconnected from everything since coming to college that I wasn't sure what place that relationship had in my new life.

excited about the Bible study. They encouraged me to come with them every week. I think they knew how much it would mean to me to hang out with that group of college students who were all in different places in their faith journeys but who came together to support each other and learn more about God.

I was really excited to see if some of my other teammates were going through some of the same things I was or had the same questions. I'd gotten closer to Jesus in high school, but I felt so disconnected from everything since coming to college that I wasn't sure what place that relationship had in my new life.

That Bible study was the first place I'd felt complete since coming to college. Right away, I felt the relief of knowing that I was in a place where it was okay to admit I didn't feel fulfilled even though I was supposedly living my dream. It was a safe place to ask difficult questions, where I was never made to feel dumb for asking them or ashamed for feeling doubt or uncertainty.

LOVE AND ACCEPTANCE

That environment of acceptance and love, I realize now, was a reflection of the love of Jesus. Those people were so full of His love that it spilled over and made me want to be part of it in a way I never had before. Regardless of how far along someone was in her journey with God, there was no sense of comparison or seniority—we were all just there to learn more about Jesus and His love for us.

I've always loved to learn, and learning with my friends and taking our hard questions to the Bible created a strong bond between us—one that was even stronger than our connection as teammates because it was based on our truest, permanent identities as God's children. I will forever be grateful for those girls and the way God used them to bring me closer to Him by finally showing me what I was missing.

I'll be the first person to tell you that having a relationship with Jesus doesn't mean all your problems are going to magically go away. Even after I saw my need for Him in my life, it took a long time for me to learn how to let Him be the center of it—and honestly, I'm still learning that lesson!

WHAT YOU DO VERSUS WHO YOU ARE

I've always been surrounded by serious soccer players. Most of the girls who played for my club growing up wanted to play in college, so they, like me, were "all soccer, all the time" kind of people. In college, all of my teammates had been working toward that goal for years, and finally, when I started playing professionally, I was surrounded by women who had made soccer their life's work.

> Those people were so full of God's love that it spilled over and made me want to be part of it in a way I never had before.

The thing about pursuing a goal with that kind of dedication and hard work, especially one that takes so much time and training, is that it becomes easy for you to confuse your *identity* with your *profession*—in other words, to think that what you *do* is who you *are*.

I've had a lot of teammates over the years who have had to stop playing because of a serious injury. The initial disappointment is bad enough, but after they've been out of the game for a while, some of them realize they don't know who they are without soccer. A few of my friends went through some dark times when they had to stop playing. All of a sudden, after years of being a soccer player, they weren't anymore, and it was easy to conclude if they couldn't play soccer, they no longer had value or purpose. After all, what good is a soccer player who can't play soccer?

"WHO AM I WITHOUT THIS?"

This isn't unique to soccer players or even athletes in general. When you get older, you'll notice that one of the first questions people will ask when they meet you is "What do you do?" or "Where do you work?" We are so in the habit of thinking about people in terms of what they "do" that we forget a person's job or profession is only one part of her.

> My sense of self-worth had to come from something besides soccer.

For a lot of soccer players I've known, however, that "soccer player" identity was the only one they invested in or spent time developing for a big portion of their lives. Don't get me wrong—having a dream or a goal is important, but the danger in basing your whole identity and sense of worth on that goal is that you eventually have to ask yourself, "Without this, who am I? Am I anyone?"

PEACE AND JOY–ON AND OFF THE FIELD

My faith answered that question for me. A couple of years into my pro career, there was a stretch of time when I felt like I wasn't playing my best. There are highs and lows in everyone's career, but I wasn't happy with my performance and was frustrated and dissatisfied. Having my identity based so strongly on what I did meant that when soccer wasn't going right, nothing felt right.

Thankfully, God helped me recognize how backward that attitude was. My sense of self-worth had to come from something besides soccer. Thanks to some of my Christian teammates and some wonderful mentors at our church, I began to see that the most important part of my identity was that I was loved by Jesus. He used the people in my life to affirm me not just as a soccer player but as the whole, unique person He'd created me to be.

> When I stopped trying to find my identity in soccer, I ended up loving the game even more and finding more joy in it than ever before.

When I finally stopped basing my identity on what I could do and instead based it on who I was in Jesus, I found lasting joy and unconditional peace on and off the field. I think God had wanted to give me that for a while, but I'd been letting soccer occupy first place in my life for a long time. The cool thing is that when I stopped trying to find my identity in soccer, I ended up loving the game even more and finding more joy in it than ever before. God gave me my love for the game, and He gave me gifts and skills that He *wants* me to use. Following Him first doesn't mean I have to give up the things He created me to love; on the contrary, it frees me to love and pursue soccer for His glory without letting it define or control me.

THE CHALLENGE OF FAITH

I think it's important to know that having faith is sometimes *really* difficult. I'm not a super patient person, and the world we live in has a lot of opportunities to quickly get what I want. Hungry? You can get a drive-through meal in a minute. Want to listen to a certain song? You can pull it up instantly on your phone. Want a delicious coffee drink custom made just for you? There's a coffee shop on every corner. I think a lot of people today have been spoiled by the convenience and speed of our lives, and they expect immediate results when they ask God for something.

I've definitely been guilty of this before. When God doesn't answer a prayer right away or how I want Him to, I can feel disappointed. Thankfully, God is always more than capable of handling our questions and our frustration, and those times of confusion and doubt can become opportunities for your faith to be strengthened.

> Having faith
> is sometimes
> *really* difficult.

"I'M SORRY, BUT YOU'RE NOT READY"

I learned this the hard way when I didn't make the qualifying team for the 2015 World Cup. I'd had disappointments as a player before—a loss when I'd expected a win, a missed penalty kick—but this was especially hard because I had wanted it *so* bad. What I wanted more than anything was to start in the World Cup, and the first step was to make the qualifying team. I went into the tryouts thinking, *I'm working hard—I'm going to get this!* But afterward, I had a conversation with the coach.

"I'm sorry, but you're not ready," she told me gently. "You definitely have potential, but you're just not there yet."

I still remember how crushed I was. I'd been dreaming of the chance to play in the World Cup for longer than I could remember, and to fall short of making the qualifying team felt like the end of that dream. What made the disappointment even worse was I knew I hadn't pushed myself hard enough to make the roster.

I prayed a lot during that time. I wasn't mad at God, but I was confused. *This doesn't make any sense*, I thought. I had wanted it so bad! I had prayed so hard for it! Why hadn't He answered my prayer? I'd felt like my World Cup dreams were going to come true, but now it felt like the world was ending—or at least, my world. When you're in the middle of something hard, it's difficult to believe in a bigger purpose, and for a while, I struggled with feelings of uncertainty and insecurity.

> When you're in the middle of something hard, it's difficult to believe in a bigger purpose.

A SECOND CHANCE

Because I'd been one of the last ones cut, I knew I was basically an alternate if anyone were to get injured. Right before the first qualifying game, one of my best friends, Crystal Dunn, hurt her knee in practice and wasn't going to be able to continue in the tournament. I was so devastated for her. I knew firsthand how disappointing it was to be so close to a goal but not reach it. When I got a call from the head coach asking if I wanted to join the team the next day to replace Crystal, my feelings were a mix of shock and excitement.

I was thankful for the opportunity to train with the team, even as an alternate, but still I was crushed—Crystal deserved to be there and couldn't be, and I did *not* deserve to be there. It was hard to take her spot knowing full well that I had fallen short of really earning it. That knowledge was really humbling and made me extra determined to make the most of that opportunity. I knew I probably wouldn't get to play, but I was

> I was going to do the best I could to strengthen the team, to prepare the starters and make them the best they could be.

going to learn. I kept telling myself I was going to do the best I could to strengthen the team, to prepare the starters and make them the best they could be.

LEARNING FROM DISAPPOINTMENT

Every minute I was with the team, my hunger to be part of it got stronger. I knew then I hadn't done enough to make the team the first time. God had answered my first prayer with a no, which I now realize was just the motivation I needed. I went from passively hoping I would be good enough to being a whole new level of determined to *get* good enough.

> It wasn't easy to hear God say no, but it taught me to be honest with myself and know my weaknesses.

Those feelings brought a drive and a fearlessness to my playing that I hadn't had before. It wasn't easy to hear God say no at the time, but it taught me to be honest with myself and know my weaknesses. If He had said yes right away, I wouldn't have had any reason to push myself to become the player I am today. I would have continued to settle, and I'm learning that God doesn't want us to settle for anything less than His best for us, even when we think we know better.

AN EVEN BIGGER DREAM

In the months leading up to the World Cup, I pushed myself harder in training than ever before. I kept telling myself, "Make the twenty-three, make the twenty-three." I didn't just want to be on the team anymore—I wanted to start. I wanted to play. When I found out I'd made the roster, it really affirmed God's control over my life. Sometimes, He doesn't give us what we want because He wants to give us something even better.

I would have been happy if God had given me the "pretty cool" version of my dream—making the qualifying team—but He didn't let me settle for that. He wanted to give me the "wildest dreams" version—making the starting roster for the World Cup—and He used my disappointment to motivate me to do the work I needed to be good enough to get there.

A CONTINUING JOURNEY

My faith is a continuing journey, and I definitely don't have it all figured out, but I have been through enough with God to know I can always bring my questions and insecurities to Him, and He will handle them. I continue to dive into His Word to get to know Him better and learn about how He wants me to live my life, and I try to spend as much time talking with Him one-on-one as I can.

If I learned anything from playing soccer for twenty years, it's that the game always goes better if you're listening to the Coach!

> Sometimes God doesn't give us what we want because He wants to give us something even better.

5

ADVERSITY

Think about one of your favorite memories—maybe a fun vacation with your family or winning a championship game. Think about all the things you loved about that experience. How great did you feel? How big was your smile that day? Really relive it and try to remember what that joy felt like.

Now think about one of the hardest times in your life. Not as much fun to remember, right? Nobody in their right mind would say "I'd love to go through that again!" No one wants to go through hard times, but the fact is, everyone's going to have some hard things come up in their lives. That's out of your control, but the good news is, you have a choice as to how you respond to it, and if you make the right choice, you'll come out stronger on the other side.

One of the most difficult, scariest things I ever went through in my life happened when I was in high school. I was only a couple years away from my college soccer goals. Our club had won the state championship the last five years in a row, and it looked like we'd be heading back for a sixth try. I had just gotten my driver's license, and I loved the freedom of driving myself. It felt like the next few years were going to be great. Looking back, it almost feels like a movie—you know, where things are going so well at the beginning that you're just sure something bad is about to happen to the poor main character?

RIVALRIES

If you play for a team or are a fan of a sport, you're probably familiar with the concept of rivalries between teams. Of course, in any game, both teams want to win and feel competitive against their opponents, but for whatever reason, certain teams and their fans develop an extracompetitive attitude. Sometimes it's because they're both from the same area, so they're competing for "territory."

Sometimes it's because they're evenly matched and have traded wins for a long time, leaving both sides hungry to claim first place. And sometimes a rivalry exists because of background drama among players or coaches or even fans.

These rivalries are usually pretty friendly—there isn't a lot of actual bad feeling on either side, just a heightened sense of competition—and the fans and players often enjoy rivalry games even more than normal games. The higher stakes make it more exciting, and the victory is sweeter.

A BAD HIT

It was the middle of a rivalry game against a team our club had been battling for years. We were all feeling the effects of that rivalry, and everyone was playing with more aggression than usual. It was a close game, and probably thirty minutes into the second half, I got on breakaway going to goal. My excitement was sky high—I had a really good play going! I was about to go one-on-one with the goalkeeper and feeling good about my chances when something hit me like a truck from the side.

I crashed to the ground, my head bouncing off the pitch. A girl from the other team had slammed into me like a linebacker. It was such a bad hit that she got a red card and was ejected from the game immediately.

My first thought after the initial shock wore off was *Aw, man!* I was bummed because I'd lost my shot at the goal, and my cool breakaway move had been wasted. My second thought upon standing back up was *Wow, that* really *hurt.* Several things were sore, but the worst pain was coming from my lower back. I'd been knocked down before,

> I crashed to the ground, my head bouncing off the pitch.

though, and now I was extra motivated to help win the game, so I kept playing. Whether it was the adrenaline or the ibuprofen, the pain faded pretty quickly, and I was able to finish the game without any trouble.

SIDELINED

Over the next few weeks, however, the pain came back—and it got worse. My back went from being a little stiff, to a *lot* stiff, to radiating pain constantly, even when I wasn't moving. It got to the point where I was having a hard time even getting myself up and out of my bed in the morning.

Things I was used to doing without thinking about them were now major ordeals. I had to totally change how I moved, and even an activity as simple pulling on pants was a problem because I couldn't bend over. I had to pile them on the floor with the legs scrunched up, put both feet through, then use a coat hanger hooked through one of the belt loops to pull them up around my hips!

I kept trying to play through the pain, which probably made it worse,

> I finally had to sit out and watch my team from the sidelines.

but I finally had to sit out and watch my team from the sidelines. That part of it was even harder to deal with, since I wanted so badly to be out there on the field.

My teammates were really encouraging, praying for me and telling me positive things like "You'll be back soon" and "You're going to be fine!" Their support meant the world to me, but as time passed and the pain didn't go away, I started to get scared that something was seriously wrong. Finally, I told my mom, "It's not getting better."

"LET'S FIGURE IT OUT"

My mom is a nurse, so her experience and medical knowledge was a big advantage to me as an athlete. She was never the mom to freak out over an injury. She was always very calm and matter-of-fact, which helped keep me calm. "Well, let's figure out what's wrong and get it taken care of," she told me, and my panic subsided a little. If Mom said we could get it taken care of, it was going to be fine.

The first doctor we went to was not very encouraging. An MRI showed that I had herniated two discs in my back, and his advice was to give it time to heal on its own. In the meantime, I would have to avoid strenuous activity. Since the pain had been getting worse as time passed, I wasn't too thrilled with this diagnosis, but my mom and I decided to try his advice.

When you play a sport at a high level, injuries are going to happen. You're putting your body through a lot, and at that age, your body is still growing and changing, which makes injuries even harder to avoid. I'd watched several friends and teammates go through injuries over the past couple of years—some of them minor, some of them serious—and as I waited to see whether my back would heal, I couldn't help but think about the friends who had to leave the sport they loved because of a career-ending injury.

"IS THIS IT?"

Time passed, and I had less pain, but my range of motion was still limited. Sick of watching from the sidelines, I started to play again, but I was only able to play at a fraction of the level I'd been at before the hit. I had to change how I played and serve a completely different role in the game. I was supposed to be a midfielder, but I was playing as

> When you play a sport at a high level, injuries are going to happen.

a center forward because pretty much all I could do was lay up balls for my team and let them take it from there.

It was really hard—I wanted to be able to do a lot more for my team, but I had to accept my limitations. And in the back of my mind, I was thinking, *Is this it? Is this going to be as much as I can ever play?* I was terrified that my dreams of college soccer were slipping away.

A NEW PERSPECTIVE

My wonderful mom was my biggest support system during that time and the main reason why I didn't completely lose hope. When the first doctor's treatment didn't accomplish anything, she started researching other doctors who specialized in sports injuries, especially back injuries like mine. We tried a couple different treatments and therapies, and when one thing wouldn't work, she encouraged me to stay positive, keep praying, and keep looking for a solution.

We finally found a doctor who suggested some shots at the injury site to reduce the inflammation, and I still remember the immediate relief I felt when he gave me the first injection. It was like all the fear and uncertainty I'd been feeling melted away with the pain.

> I had a new appreciation for what a gift it was to be able to play and to work hard at something I loved.

When I finally got back to playing full out without pain, I was so grateful to be back on the field and feeling like myself again. After having to face the possibility of giving up soccer, I had a new appreciation for what a gift it was to be able to play and to work hard at something I loved. That injury and time off gave me a new perspective on things that had felt hard or painful before.

After my recovery, I never complained about anything—not a tough warm-up, not sore muscles, not being tired. I was just so happy to be back. That was a lasting benefit of my injury: I learned to never take my health or my opportunities for granted because of how quickly circumstances can change. That's a big reason I do everything in my power to play every minute of every game as full out and on fire as possible. You never know how many minutes you have left in your career!

COMING BACK BETTER

I always try to tell young girls that you can react to adversity one of two ways—either by quitting and giving up or by pushing through it and letting it make you not just a better athlete but a better person. There's almost always something you can learn or a way you can grow when life is really hard.

When I wasn't able to play, I spent a lot of time watching and learning from the game. Was that as fun as playing? Of course not! But because I wasn't just sitting there feeling sorry for myself, I came out of that experience with a better understanding of the game, my team's strengths, and how we worked together, and I know I came back a better player because of it.

> Adversity can make you not just a better athlete but a better person.

ADVERSITY AND HONESTY

I've also learned how important it is to be honest with yourself and with the people around you about how you're feeling when you're going through hard times. Yes, you can try your best to keep up a positive attitude, but there will still be dark moments when you feel like nothing will ever be okay again, and when you can't imagine feeling better.

Those are the times when it's so important to have people around you whom you can trust with your true heart, like a parent, friend, coach, or teammate. Throughout the whole ordeal with my back, I was honest with my mom about

> I was honest with my mom about my feelings because I knew if I wasn't, those fears and doubts would eat me up inside.

my feelings because I knew if I wasn't, those fears and doubts would eat me up inside. To be able to say out loud to her "I'm really afraid I'll never be the player I was again" meant that I wasn't carrying the burden of that fear alone. I can't imagine how I would have survived without being able to be vulnerable with my family and my teammates.

ADVERSITY AND COMPASSION

Going through hard times of my own also means I have compassion for others when things go wrong in their lives. My older sister, Melanie, was one of the players I watched walk away from soccer because of some major injuries. I remember how hard it was seeing her get hurt again and again, how she tried to push through, and how she gradually had to accept what her body was telling her.

Melanie was my first and closest competitor—the person whose trail I had always followed—and suddenly she wasn't going to be able to play the sport we both loved. I was worried that my still being able to play would make her sad or that she would resent me for being on the field when she had to watch from the sidelines. I was nervous that we weren't going to have the same relationship anymore, but it actually made us a lot closer.

I was able to empathize with her disappointment and uncertainty because I'd felt those same emotions when I injured my back. At the same time, she knew she could be real and vulnerable with me about how she was feeling as she tried to figure out what she wanted to do with her life after soccer, and we both learned how to continue to push and support each other.

> It's important not to minimize one person's struggles just because they don't seem as bad as yours.

IT MATTERS

Adversity can take on many forms depending on your circumstances. Moving to a new city, watching your parents go through a divorce, giving up something you love because money is tight, suffering from a major illness or injury—these are all real and legitimate hardships to the people going through them, and it's important not to minimize one person's struggles just because they don't seem as bad as yours.

Battling cancer and battling a school bully are both scary fights. We should all try to keep a healthy perspective on our own hardships and remember even though they are no fun, they can help us grow stronger. And even in the most difficult times, we can also remember that we have a lot of things to be thankful for.

6

LOOKING UP

Have you ever watched one of those montage videos of people walking and looking at their phones at the same time? You have to feel sorry for them when they run into light posts or step into fountains, but at the same time, you want to call out, "Watch where you're going!" It's common sense that you should be looking ahead to help you get where you want to go.

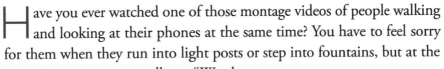

Throughout my life, I've been blessed to have many amazing role models.

"Watch where you're going" is actually a pretty good philosophy for life in general. If you want to achieve a goal, one of the best things you can do is look ahead at the people who've gone before you and are already where you want to go. You might call them "role models" or "heroes," but whatever you call them, having those people to look up to and learn from makes it easier to reach your goals.

A role model is someone we "model" ourselves after—or try to be like in certain ways—and having great role models is an important part of becoming the people we want to become and achieving the goals we set for ourselves. Throughout my life, I've been blessed to have many amazing role models.

REMINDERS OF WHAT'S POSSIBLE

No one will be surprised to learn that my bedroom walls were covered with posters of soccer players when I was growing up. I literally "looked up" at those pictures of Mia Hamm, Brandi Chastain, Shannon MacMillan, and so many others every single day. My Women's National Team poster was one of my most prized possessions, but the thing that made me hang those posters on my wall wasn't how cool the pictures were or how much I liked the uniforms. Those pictures were a constant reminder of what was possible if I kept working hard and doing my best.

My pro career was still ten years off, and I didn't have any guarantee that I'd even be good enough to play in college—much less in the World Cup—but that didn't stop me from looking at these incredible, hardworking, strong women and dreaming. There were nights when I'd come home from practice, sweaty and exhausted, muscles screaming, eyes blurry, knowing I'd have to wake up for school way too soon. When I found myself wondering whether all my hard work was going to amount to anything, I'd see those posters and feel a little less alone. If those women had made it through the late-night practices and sore muscles, maybe I could too.

> If those women had made it through the late-night practices and sore muscles, maybe I could too.

A HERO IN REAL LIFE

I consider myself lucky in that I got to meet some of my heroes while I was young. When I was fourteen, I was invited to a soccer camp sponsored by U.S. Soccer, where they gave one hundred of the best players under age fourteen from across the country the chance to train, play, and hear from some major coaches and pro players.

> My first heroes were the women closest to me: my mom and my older sister.

When I got the invitation, I was really nervous but also thrilled at the opportunity. I remember being at the camp the first night and sitting in the second row of the auditorium packed with other girls like me. Up on the stage was Shannon MacMillan, World Cup champion and Olympic gold medalist, and all of us looked up at her like we couldn't quite believe we were in the same room. All I could think was, *I have a poster of this woman on my wall!*

Experiences like that really helped keep my goals in view. A poster is a great reminder, but hearing from one of my heroes in person made them that much more real to me—and made me even more motivated to follow in women like Shannon's footsteps.

HEROES AT HOME

Not all my role models have been famous or even soccer players. When I was growing up, women's sports weren't shown on TV as often as they are now, so I didn't know a lot about women's pro soccer until I got to middle school. My first heroes were actually the women closest to me: my mom and my older sister.

My mom is the most supportive, positive person I could imagine having in my corner, and even when I was little, I recognized how much I could learn from her about caring for people, taking responsibility for myself, and doing what needs to be done without complaining or expecting a reward.

My sister was, in my opinion, the coolest. She was really good at everything we did when we were younger, and most of the things I did that probably drove her crazy—like borrowing her clothes or following her into every sport she tried—I did because I wanted to be just like her. (So older sibs, remember that when your little siblings are bugging you, and remember how much they admire you!) She was the one who went first in everything, who had already tried everything I wanted to try, and who was bigger and faster than I was (at least until I outgrew her). Having her so close and yet two years ahead of me in most things made her the best role model I could have had for all the important things you have to learn growing up, like how to survive in a new school or new class and how to get along with your parents.

> I'm pretty sure it was all those years of trying to keep up with Melanie that pushed me to that higher level.

My sister was also as crazy about sports as I was, especially soccer, so growing up right behind her meant I always had someone to play with. And because she was bigger and better than I was, I had to work harder to keep up with her.

When I'd been playing for my club for a while, I was asked to "play up," which meant they wanted me to play on a team with girls who were a year older than I was. I'm pretty sure it was all those years of trying to keep up with Melanie that pushed me to that higher level, so thanks, Mel!

MAKING LEARNING FUN

My coaches have obviously been some of the biggest influences in my life. They taught me about the game, teamwork, and sportsmanship, and they helped me learn about myself as a player and a person. I'm so thankful for the role each of them has played in my career. I have my earliest coaches to thank for making soccer practice a place where I felt excited to be learning a new skill while still giving us really young players the freedom to be creative with it, even when we weren't playing perfectly.

My first club is where I really fell in love with the game, and that was because the coach made learning it so much fun. It wasn't about what you were doing wrong—it was about learning how to do it better. Trying out new skills and strategies was fun because I was learning alongside my friends, and because the emphasis was on improvement and not perfection, it made it easy to love playing rather than get frustrated when we didn't win.

TEAM, TEAM, TEAM

A big reason we switched to Sereno Soccer Club when I was twelve was because of their coaching model. At Sereno, you had to switch coaches every two years as you progressed as a player. I loved this policy. Every coach has her own methods and her own list of things to teach you, so when you learn from a variety of people, it makes sense that you're going to learn a lot.

My first coach at Sereno, Paul Lester, loved to teach the game of soccer as a whole. He really wanted us to appreciate the big picture, breaking down different styles of playing, explaining the use of different formations, and especially teaching us how to function as a team. "Team, team, team"— that's what I remember most about Paul's coaching.

He showed us how cool it is when the individual members of a team work as a unit. He demonstrated how much the person next to you on the field means to what you're doing, and that connection between players is still one of the things I love most about the game.

DISCIPLINE AND DRIVE

After Paul came Jason Goodson. Paul had cultivated my love of working as a team, and now Jason focused on the individual. His coaching was all about how to increase my individual skill as a player—how much faster I could run, how good I could be on the ball, how accurate my shooting was, and so on.

As fourteen- and fifteen-year-olds, my teammates and I were figuring out the people we were going to become, so this type of approach to the game fit right in. Everyone was ready to learn what her special skills and strengths were and how to develop them. By putting a lot of time into our individual crafts and strengths and addressing our weaknesses, we played better when we united on the field.

> Your role models don't have to be older than you.

My last two years at Sereno were spent under Head Coach Les Armstrong. Les was a big reason Sereno had a reputation for helping players meet their college goals—he was the coach who made you a college player. Les was probably the toughest of all my youth coaches, but at that age—when I was starting to look ahead to college and question what I wanted to accomplish as a player—I needed that extra push. Through those intense workouts, my vision for my future in the game came into sharper focus, thanks in large part to the drive and the discipline Les instilled in me.

FRIENDS AS HEROES

Your role models don't have to be older than you either. I've known my friend Sarah since we were thirteen. We played soccer together growing up and all through college, and she has influenced me just as much as any of those women on the soccer posters.

Sarah's whole approach to life is full of energy and positivity. She sees life as a fun party God is throwing to show people how much He loves them, and she's helping Him host it! People are drawn to Sarah like a magnet. She has an amazing gift of making everyone she meets feel important, and as long as I've known her, I've tried to be like her in that way.

> Having people who were willing to include me and listen to me was a huge blessing when I was still trying to figure out who I was and what I wanted out of life.

Sarah is still a person I continue to look to as an example of how to be a truly great friend. Whatever season I'm in—whether it's high or low—she's always there for me, is willing to help with whatever I need, and is great at helping me look at the bigger picture when things aren't going well. She brings out the best in me, and that's the definition of a good role model.

SOCCER TEAM MOMS

I didn't stop looking up to role models and heroes when I got older. When I went to college, I had a tough time adjusting to being away from my family. We had spent so much time together when I was growing up, and now I was seven hundred miles away from them in California. Michelle was a Santa Clara alum who volunteered in the soccer program and was basically our soccer team mom. Her best friend, Jodi, coached at a nearby club while also working with the Santa Clara team, and both of these unbelievable women have been huge influences in my life, both in and after college.

Jodi and Michelle became my second family while I was in college, investing one of the most important things in the world in me: time. They took time out of their own schedules to be there for me in a difficult transitional period. Having people who were willing to include me and listen to me was a huge blessing when I was still trying to figure out who I was and what I wanted out of life. They gave me a safe space to be vulnerable about how I was feeling and to ask for help when I needed it, and more important than anything else, they made me laugh! Showing me how to find the joy in everything was a lesson that I have been thankful for every day.

HEROES BIG AND SMALL

Even as an adult, I try to be mindful about surrounding myself with positive examples to follow. Life is a journey, and you're never done growing and improving and becoming the person God wants to you be, so why would you stop looking for people to help you get there? Some of the biggest influences in Zach's and my life together have been the pastors at our church in New Jersey. They have lifted us up in some of the hardest times of our lives while challenging us to cultivate a closer walk with the Lord and lead a life that reflects Him.

I'll say it again because I believe it so strongly: *Time* is one of the greatest gifts you can give someone, and Pastors Kyle and Danielle have had a major impact in our lives because of their willingness to invest their time. They walk with us on our journey, make us feel valuable, and show us an endless amount of selfless love. Through my highs and lows,

> I try to be mindful about surrounding myself with positive examples to follow.

they are there to support me and lift me up. Zach and I have been inspired by the way they share their hearts, and we try to model ourselves after them in that way. I admire their honesty, vulnerability, and generosity every day.

Some of my biggest heroes are the Make-A-Wish kids who visit our team. The Women's National Team frequently works with the Make-A-Wish Foundation to grant "wishes" to kids who are facing life-threatening medical conditions.

It's amazing to me that these boys and girls want nothing more than to meet and play soccer with our team. They are so young, yet they bravely face some really scary diseases and unpleasant treatments. And they even find joy in life by spending a little time with us and watching us play! These things are immensely humbling, and they remind me to live my life to the fullest and to make the most out of the platform I have to serve others.

Before Wish Kids visit, we read about them, their stories, and their families. We get to hang out with them for only a little bit—taking photos when they come to training, or even playing with them a little if they're able to—and then we host them at a game. The courage and determination these kids have are like nothing I've seen before, and I don't know a single player who isn't inspired by them every time.

FIND SOMEONE TO LOOK UP TO

I really don't know where I would be today—or even who I would be today—without the examples set for me by so many people who have inspired me to be like them in some way. If you're looking for a surefire way to get closer to your goals and dreams, find the people in your life who are worth looking up to. If you want to get better at something, look at who's ahead of you. For me, that was my older sister, the Arizona State University (ASU) women's team, and the pros on my posters. Role models can be those who are way ahead of you on the path, or they can be just a couple steps in front. What are they doing right? Whom do you admire, and what sets them apart?

Another piece of advice I like to pass on is to think about where you want to be in five years and then look at who's already there. That might be high school or college girls, depending on your age right now, and if you're in high school or college, that might be women playing their first year for a pro team. Ask yourself (or your role models, if you have the chance) the same questions: What are they doing that's working? What habits do they have that you might want to be forming now? What makes them stand out?

> If you're looking for a surefire way to get closer to your goals and dreams, find the people in your life who are worth looking up to.

You can build a template with this information to plot your own path. No one's journey is going to look exactly the same, but it never hurts to have a map to consult when you're deciding which path to take.

Heroes and role models show us a hopeful picture of the future to hang on to when the present seems hard. I love the competitive aspect of soccer and the drive to improve, but without my role models, I don't know if I would have kept going when I couldn't see the future clearly. I don't think being good at soccer, or even loving it, would have been enough to make me persevere through those difficult times.

(ALMOST) NO ONE IS PERFECT

The last thing I'll say about heroes is that it's important to remember that no one is perfect. Everyone you look up to is human, and that means they can make mistakes or disappoint you just like anyone else. When they do, it can be hard to accept, and sometimes you might feel personally hurt when your heroes stumble or fall short of your expectations.

That's why I try to look to Jesus as the best possible example to follow. He *is* perfect, and He will never let you down, so you can't go wrong modeling yourself after Him! Now that I'm a role model for so many young athletes, I look to my earthly heroes as well as Jesus to inspire me to be a person worth looking up to.

7

PERSPECTIVE AND POSITIVITY

am not a person who keeps her feelings a secret. You can ask anyone who knows me, and they'll agree I do *not* believe in holding your emotions inside! That means everyone can tell pretty quickly when I'm upset or angry (my mom calls it "the wrath of Julie"), but most of the time, the emotion I'm projecting is happiness. People are always telling me, "You are such a positive person! What is your secret?"

Obviously, I don't feel happy *all* the time—I have good and bad days just like anybody else—but I do think I've learned a lot about how to have a positive attitude in just about every situation. My "secret," if you want to call it that, is in learning to look at things from the right perspective.

"Perspective" is the way you look at a situation. Your perspective determines whether you see an ice cream cone as a circle or a triangle—if you look at it from directly overhead, it's a circle; if you look at it from the side, it's a triangle. The distance between the object you are observing and where you're standing also affects how you see it.

You might have seen super close-up pictures of things like a penny, a butterfly wing, or a piece of bread. Those pictures are hard to recognize for what they are because you can't see the whole object. There's an old parable about some blind men who come across an elephant. Each man touches one part of the elephant—like the tail, the ear, and the trunk—and so they all think the elephant is a different thing. The man who touched the ear thought it was a fan, the man who touched the trunk thought it was a snake, and so on. None of them had all the information, so they couldn't identify the whole animal.

> Sometimes the right perspective can even make negative things seems like positive ones!

ADJUSTING YOUR PERSPECTIVE

If I have a positive attitude most of the time, it's because I've learned how important your perspective is to understanding what happens to you and how you react to it. There's a way to look at just about every situation that will make it seem less discouraging, more fun, or just not as significant. Sometimes the right perspective can even make negative things seems like positive ones! The trick is to learn to adjust your perspective.

One of my favorite ways to adjust my perspective is to try to find the humor in a situation. I love to laugh, and I decided pretty early in life that I'd rather embrace humor and fun than live in a constant state of worrying about what people were thinking or whether I looked dumb.

Think about your most embarrassing moment for a minute. (Sorry if that was painful!) Whatever it was, you might have heard people say, "Oh, you'll laugh about that someday." Depending on how long ago and how embarrassing it was, they might be right or they might not be, but it is true that choosing to see the humor in a situation can make it seem a lot less disastrous!

HUMOR HELPS!

Having the right perspective saved me on my first day of middle school. Where I went to school in Arizona, middle school included seventh, eighth, and ninth graders all in the same school. That meant I would be moving from a school we shared with first graders to school we shared with ninth graders. *Big* difference! When I was in seventh grade, the ninth graders looked huge to me. They were much taller and seemed way more mature, so I and the other seventh graders were more than a little intimidated by them.

Like all first days at a new school, my first day was full of new faces and involved figuring out how to navigate a new building. Middle school was also the first time I had to travel from room to room every class period and had a different teacher for each subject. If that wasn't stressful enough, the school played warning music near the end of each passing period, which meant you had one minute from the start of the music to get to your next class or you'd be late.

Halfway through my first day, I was still looking helplessly around for my next class when the warning music started. I panicked! I had no idea where I was supposed to be. Freaking out, I picked a direction and ran through an open classroom door and flopped down in a desk just as the music finished.

Yes! I thought. *Made it!* And then I looked around. Everyone in that room was *clearly* in ninth grade, and most of them were staring at me. I probably turned bright pink—at least, that's my guess from how hot my face felt. The teacher was saying something, the class was starting, and I was definitely in the wrong place.

For a second, I was frozen in my seat, not wanting to face the humiliation of drawing even more attention to myself by admitting I was lost. (Although, even in my panic, I couldn't help but notice that, hey, some of those ninth-grade boys were pretty cute—maybe the situation wasn't all bad!) After another second, I came to my senses and knew I couldn't go undercover as a ninth grader the rest of the year.

> What I could have seen as a humiliating, horrible experience was now a funny story my friends and I would talk about all day, and the difference was all in how I looked at it.

And suddenly I was cracking up at the whole ridiculous situation—the way I'd sprinted in a random direction when the music started, my short seventh-grade self surrounded by giant ninth graders—and I thought, *Oh, well, might as well get it over with!* I sheepishly raised my hand. The teacher broke off whatever she'd been saying and looked a little annoyed to be interrupted.

"Yes?" she asked.

"Um, if this isn't seventh-grade social studies, I'm lost," I said.

The teacher chuckled, and so did most of the rest of the room, but now that I had chosen to laugh at myself, the laughs felt friendly rather than mean, and I actually kind of enjoyed having the spotlight in that room full of ninth graders as the teacher explained exactly where I was supposed to be and how to get there. I had to walk to a totally different part of the school and made a grand entrance into the right class by walking in five minutes after the door had been closed.

Earlier in the day, I'd been a ball of nerves, but now I was laughing at my trip to ninth-grade geometry and couldn't wait to tell my friends the whole ridiculous story. We all had a big laugh about it, and they were jealous I'd gotten the chance to check out the ninth-grade boys. What I could have seen as a humiliating, horrible experience was now a funny story my friends and I would talk about all day, and the difference was all in how I looked at it.

THE PERSPECTIVE OF TIME

Another thing that can really affect your perspective is time. Things that seem huge and significant one day often fade pretty quickly, and a week or even a day later, you feel very differently than you did in the middle of the situation. Your own maturity and experience also change over time, so it's important not to judge things or people on your first impressions or to hold grudges, since your new perspective might be totally different.

Remember the soccer camp I went to at Santa Clara University? The one I *hated*? Even though the experience helped me grow as a player and a person, my twelve-year-old self hated it, my thirteen-year-old self hated it, my fourteen-year-old self remembered hating it, and—well, you get the idea. Fast-forward to the end of my sophomore year in high school. I was getting all these letters and offers to play for different college soccer teams, and I had no idea where I wanted to go. I went on about ten visits to try to find the school that felt right, but I didn't have strong feelings for any of them. Then one day when I came home from school, my mom held up an envelope.

"Who's that from?" I asked, not looking at it very closely.

She grinned. "You'll never guess—Santa Clara, your favorite place!" Still smiling, she handed me the letter.

I glared at the Santa Clara logo and then tore open the envelope. The assistant coach had written me a personal

> It's important not to judge things or people on your first impressions or to hold grudges, since your new perspective might be totally different.

letter expressing the coaches' interest in me and saying he would love for me to visit and check out the school.

Not in a million years! I thought and chucked the letter onto a pile of junk mail. No way was I going back to that place! Never mind that my bad experience hadn't really had anything to do with the college itself or the campus or that one of my best friends had already committed to the school—I just remembered how miserable I had been, and because I'd been thinking about that camp as a horrible place for the past five years, I saw no reason to even consider it.

> Time changes the way you see things.

When I got to practice the next day, a bunch of my friends were standing in a group talking about college options.

"Julie!" one of them called, pulling me over to the group. "We're talking about Santa Clara! Have you looked at it yet?"

"Uh, yeah, it's on my list," I said. I didn't want to kill her excitement, but in my head I was thinking, *How much could it have changed?* It didn't surprise me they were talking about it; four older girls who had played for our club were currently playing at Santa Clara, but I still had no interest in revisiting the most miserable experience of my life every day of my college career.

More time passed, and my mom kept gently suggesting that maybe I should go ahead and visit Santa Clara, just so I could say I'd explored all my options. I finally agreed, more to make her happy than anything else, and once more flew out to California by myself. Five hours into my visit, I called my mom and said, "This is it. This is my school."

From the moment I stepped onto the campus, I knew Santa Clara was where I wanted to go to college. It was like that camp had happened in another lifetime. I loved the campus, I loved the area, I adored the coach, and the team felt like family, with all the girls who had played for my club.

I still laugh every time I think about how much I hated my first trip to the school I ended up loving. But that just proves my point about perspective: Time changes the way you see things. As you grow and mature, so do your views and your preferences, so you should keep an open mind about people and experiences you might have had a problem with in the past—or that negativity might lock you out of some great opportunities.

A PERSPECTIVE ON FAILURE

A change in perspective can make the biggest difference when you fail. Don't get me wrong—failure is not fun, and I've never met anyone who thought it was. But trying new things is *really* fun. I've always thought so, and the thing about trying new things is, you rarely do something perfectly the first time. In fact, you usually fail. It makes sense: You've never done it before, so how would you know how to do it perfectly?

My parents taught me to see failure as something that automatically goes along with the fun of trying new things. It's the price you have to pay. Now I always take the thrill of exploring something new over my dislike of failure.

I think it's important that young people learn it's okay to fail. Our culture has made people so scared to fail that when they do, it feels like the worst possible thing that could have happened. My

> Shifting your perspective to see failure as an opportunity to learn and grow makes all the difference in your attitude.

mom and dad taught me to respond to failure by asking "Okay, what can I learn from that?" or "What would I do differently next time?" So many people respond to failure by shutting down, but shifting your perspective to see failure as an opportunity to learn and grow makes all the difference in your attitude.

"YOU'RE DONE COMPLAINING"

When I was ten, my sister and I got mountain bikes for Christmas. My bike was a little too big for me. It was okay around the neighborhood, but my legs were short enough that my toes just barely grazed the pedals, and I had to stop and start and wobble around a lot in order to stay in motion.

After Melanie and I got used to the bikes, Dad took us to some actual mountain bike trails. It was awful! In order to push the pedals down hard enough to make it up a hill, I had to stand up on them, but that made me lose my balance, and I'd wobble. After a few minutes, Melanie and Dad were way ahead of me, and I was furious at being beaten by my older sister yet again. I finally got some speed and had a little fun going down a hill, but halfway up the other side, my momentum ran out, I scraped for the pedal with my toe but couldn't push it down, and I promptly fell over.

When Dad came back to check on me, I was biting my lip to keep from crying. I was so frustrated—my sister was just *flying* up the hill, and all I could think was, *It's not fair!* I complained through a few more hills, miserable and mad, until Dad had enough. I remember him taking me aside and saying, "Look, Julie, not everything in life is going to be easy. I'm sorry you're not having fun, but you're done complaining!"

Now when I go back home, I train on those hills, and I actually *sprint* up them. After struggling so much there when I was young, it's turned into one of my favorite places to be. At the end of the trail, there's a big boulder where people have graffitied their names. The last time I ran there, I noticed someone had added the name "Julie" to that rock, and even though

I know it must have been another Julie, seeing that name makes it feel like it's _my_ mountain.

I love the idea that the "hills" in life that seem huge and impossible to surmount in the moment might be the same hills you fly up and down years later when you're so much stronger. Try to keep that perspective in mind when your legs are too short for the pedals—you're going to keep growing, and you're going to get better at hard things!

> You can always find something to be happy about or thankful for, even after a disappointment.

FIND SOMETHING TO BE THANKFUL FOR

Probably the most cliché advice about looking at things from a positive perspective is "Every cloud has a silver lining." This means that when things seem dark and gray like a cloudy day, there's always some little good thing to hold on to, like how the sun shines from behind the clouds, making the edges look silver. I don't usually think of it in those terms, but it's true you can always find something to be happy about or thankful for, even after a disappointment.

When I was twelve, my club won the state championship and got to go to Hawaii for the regional tournament, where we were eliminated. Fresh off the excitement of the state championship, the loss that took us out of the running for regionals was especially hard. It was the biggest-stakes game I had ever played, and I was devastated. It was supposed to be this amazing adventure with my club and my family, and now it felt like the whole trip had been a waste.

My parents weren't going to stand for that. It was just one loss! I'd lost games before, they pointed out.

"But this was regionals! It's different!" I protested.

"There will be plenty of other big games," my dad said. "But right now, we're in Hawaii, and we're going to enjoy it!"

> You have to look at the big picture to put one loss in perspective with all the opportunities and other games that are still ahead of you.

I remember feeling like nothing was ever going to be fun again, but of course, Dad was right. My family had such a great time over the next few days that it wasn't long before the loss was in my rearview mirror, hurting less with every pineapple float I ate when we toured the Dole plantation and every wave I caught when we went surfing.

Hawaii is an amazing place, and exploring it with my family made me realize that even after you lose a game, there is so much more to explore and experience in life. If you only look at the loss, you'll spend your time in Hawaii moping in the hotel room instead of hiking to a waterfall. You have to look at the big picture to put one loss in perspective with all the opportunities and other games that are still ahead of you.

THE BEST PERSPECTIVE

The biggest perspective shift of all happens when I remember that ultimately, I'm playing for God, and in the end, all that matters is that I do my best for Him on and off the field. There are so many highs and lows in pro sports, I'd go crazy if I wasn't able to look at the lows in a positive light and step back and see the big picture.

Losses and embarrassing moments and pedals that are too far to reach are always going to be a part of life, but if you look at them from the right perspective, you can respond to a negative situation with a positive attitude.

8

SACRIFICE

can't, I have soccer." I should probably put those words on a T-shirt—I would have gotten a lot of use out of it over the last fourteen years. Growing up, I gave up a lot of other experiences and activities to make room for soccer. After-school clubs? I can't, I have practice. Weekend birthday party? Wish I could, but I have a game. Youth group retreats? Sorry, out-of-town tournament. You get the idea. If it wasn't happening on the soccer field, I probably couldn't make it.

The concept of sacrifice, or giving something up so you can gain something else, isn't one that immediately makes sense to most kids, and it's definitely not one that sounds fun. Some people's gut reaction might be to say "You want me to give up something I like? No way!" or "I have to choose one thing instead of all of them? No, thank you."

WE WANT TO HAVE IT ALL

Those reactions are totally natural. We've all seen some version of this scenario: A little kid is standing in the toy aisle. His mom holds up two toys and asks, "Which one do you want?" The kid looks from toy to toy for a second, then grabs both of them. That kid is all of us—we want to do everything, we want to have it all, and a lot of messages seem to be telling us we can. After all, aren't they always saying in school that you can be anything you want to be?

> The key is balance— you have to make sure you're still enjoying all those activities.

I think a lot of kids hear that message and say, "Okay, then, I want to be a violinist / dancer / swimmer / basketball player / debate team member!" They make themselves and their parents, teachers, and coaches crazy by doing five things that inevitably conflict, so they end up missing their violin lesson to play in a basketball game or coming late to swim team because debate club meets at the same time. Ultimately, they get burned out and don't fully enjoy doing any of the activities.

Now, if you're one of those people who does a million activities and you've figured out a way to make it work, good for you! I actually believe kids *should* do as many things as they enjoy doing and can make time for so they don't get burned out on one thing. But the key is balance— you have to make sure you're still enjoying all those activities. And as you figure out which things you are most passionate about, you may have to make sacrifices in one area in order to reach your full potential in another.

I'm not saying one path is better than another, but every person I know who has found great success in his or her field has made that field a priority at some point. My parents and coaches taught me early on that if you really love something and feel strongly about accomplishing your goals, you have to make sacrifices.

FRIENDS WHO UNDERSTAND—OR DON'T

Like I said, in middle and high school, most people knew that if I was out of school or not at a party, I was probably playing soccer. Most of the time, that was fine with me. I loved soccer, and many of my best friends were on my team, so even when I was missing school activities or parties, I was having a great time anyway.

There were a few things that were harder to give up, though. I didn't go to a lot of school dances, and I never went to homecoming. I was always away at a tournament. I'd always thought of school dances as one of the "cool" things you got to do in middle school and high school, so missing out on those experiences—picking out a dress, getting ready with your friends, having your hair and nails done—was disappointing. Believe me, I had a twinge or two of regret when my friends talked about their dresses while I packed up for another tournament.

> I was blessed to have some great friends who were understanding about the limited time I had to spend with them.

I also felt bad when I had to miss friends' birthday parties or performances. I didn't so much regret not being able to go to the event itself, but I was sad when I couldn't be there for my friends to help celebrate them or support them and make them feel special. I was blessed to have some great friends who were understanding about the limited time I had to spend with them. That's a big reason why athletes' best friends are often their teammates—people who understand the sacrifices and limitations because they are just as committed to the same goal.

COMPETING AT SCHOOL—OR NOT

Another thing I chose to give up to meet my goals was the chance to play high school soccer. Some clubs let their players play for both club and school teams, but there are always conflicts between practice schedules and games, and our team made a decision to be fully committed to the club. It wasn't that we thought we were better than the school teams—our club played at a lot of tournaments that were scouted by college and U.S. Soccer coaches, and we knew everyone's best chance of playing her best in front of those coaches was to practice and play together consistently.

That choice was especially tough because there was a lot of pressure at my school for athletes to play for the school teams. There was prestige in representing your school through sports—and here I was with this reputation of being a serious soccer player, and I was choosing not to be part of my school's team. There might have been some negative comments about that from a few people, but honestly, I just didn't listen. I knew for me personally, playing high school soccer wasn't the right move.

I admit, though, I was tempted. I had a lot of school spirit, and I liked the idea of getting more involved by doing something I loved, but part of me had to ask, "What will I get from this? Will this help me accomplish my goals?" The honest answer was no, the high school team wouldn't give me the same level of intensity in my training or the same kind of exposure to college opportunities that my club team would, so if I was serious about my goals, there was really only one choice.

SACRIFICE AS AN EXCHANGE

I know we all hate to choose between things we love, but I've learned that having to make those hard choices, having to give up one thing in order to have another, makes you that much more on fire for the thing you choose to pursue. If I was going to miss out on a birthday party to be at practice, I was going to work my butt off during training so I would have something to show for it.

> Having to give up one thing in order to have another makes you that much more on fire for the thing you choose to pursue.

If I was going to choose a game over the homecoming dance, I was going to try my hardest to win to make sure I got something in exchange for what I'd sacrificed. If I was going to choose club soccer over high school soccer because I wanted to play in college, I was going to make the most of every chance to be seen by college coaches. Having to make tough decisions instead of taking it for granted that you can do everything forces you to appreciate the opportunities you have and be intentional about your goals.

I think it's important to point out the difference between "sacrifice" and "deprivation." Deprivation means you've been denied something you want and you don't get anything in return. Sacrifice, on the other hand, is an *exchange*. It's easy for that distinction to get lost—to think of sacrifice and say, "Oh, that's when I have to give up all these things I want." If you're doing something you *really* love, or working toward a goal you *really* want to achieve, sacrifice has a payoff that makes it worth it.

THANKS, MOM AND DAD!

Learning how to make sacrifices is not easy, especially for a kid. I was extremely blessed growing up to have my parents set the best possible example of what it looked like to sacrifice for your goals or, more important, for other people. My mom and dad were always supportive of whatever Melanie and I wanted to do. When we both discovered we loved soccer, they dove into that world—no questions asked—to help and support us however they could. For us, soccer was a full-family affair.

Soccer is expensive! Besides the cost of playing for a club, there are shoes, gear, travel expenses, and any extra coaching or training you might want to pursue. (Not to mention the cost of feeding two starving girls after every practice.) My parents worked incredibly hard to give us the best experiences and opportunities they could.

> My parents worked incredibly hard to give us the best experiences and opportunities they could.

When Melanie and I were we were fourteen and twelve, Mom and Dad started to talk to us about switching from our local club to one more than an hour's drive away from where we lived.

"Sereno's the best club in the state," I remember Dad saying, "but it's not close by, as you know."

"And it's definitely more expensive than your current club," added Mom.

Dad nodded. "But we can make it work if you really want to pursue soccer seriously."

We both did, so the switch to Sereno was made. My dad took on more hours, and my mom started a new job with a schedule that worked better for our practices and games. Every day after school we'd make the hour-plus drive to Phoenix, where Melanie and I would have back-to-back practices until 9:30. Then we'd start the long drive home. Most nights we got home around 11:00, and my parents both had to work the next day. They did this every day without a single complaint, though I'm sure they would have rather had their evenings free after working all day.

When you see someone making so many sacrifices for you, it makes you want to be a good steward of their gift. Knowing how much our parents wanted us to have those opportunities—and seeing firsthand the sacrifices they had to make for us to have them—Melanie and I never took any of it for granted.

Every time we went to practice or a game, we took it seriously and tried to get the most out of it. We knew our parents were making those sacrifices so we could have the best chance to do what we loved, and we tried to be continuously grateful.

MAKING THE MOST OF THE SACRIFICE

After watching my parents give up so much for me, I wanted to give back to them in some way. As I got older, I realized the best way to do that would be to get a soccer scholarship to college. Getting my own funding for college felt like a way to show them soccer wasn't just something I'd been doing for the fun of it—it was a dream I wanted to pursue as far as I could.

Another reason I felt so strongly about going to college was that my parents talked a lot about the importance of getting an education and all the opportunities that go along with having one. My dad especially inspired me to work toward that goal. He had always wanted to go to college but ended up leaving a few years into it and never finished his degree. I felt like it would complete his dream if I went.

Getting soccer scholarships became a driving goal for my sister and me. When I was in high school, there was no way of knowing a professional league for women would be starting up in a few years. As far as I knew, college might be the last step I could take with soccer, and I loved the idea that I might earn a scholarship and be able to tell my parents, "Look! Look what I did with the chance you gave me."

SACRIFICING ONE DREAM FOR ANOTHER

Ironically, college also became something I had to sacrifice when I started my pro career. I was drafted to the Chicago Red Stars in January of my senior year, so I had to leave school before completing my degree. It was a really tough decision, considering all the time I spent working toward my goal and everything my degree represented for me. But sometimes you have to give up something you want in order to get something else you want even more. My dream to play professional soccer had fully taken shape in college, and so when the chance came along to do that, I took it.

> Sometimes you have to give up something you want in order to get something else you want even more.

I don't want to make it sound like any of the sacrifices or choices I've made were easy—because they weren't! When you're facing a choice between two things you really want, making a decision can feel overwhelming, and the fear of making the wrong call can make you second-guess yourself. I try to take my time with important decisions, and I talk to the people closest to me about them.

At the end of the day, I make the decision for myself, but I value the wisdom of the people I trust. I'm a big believer in following my heart, which means I believe God gives me peace at a deep level when I've made a good decision, so paying attention to that feeling helps keep me from second-guessing myself after I've made a hard choice.

THE PAYOFF

When a sacrifice feels extra tough and I'm tempted to wonder if it was really worth it, I think of the moments when sacrifice has paid off big-time.

My first game as a professional player was the season opener, and I was still having a hard time believing I was actually playing for a pro league. Just four months earlier, I'd been studying for my finals, and now I was about to play professional soccer like ten-year-old me had put on all those "What do you want to be when you grow up?" assignments. I had a starting spot, and my team was playing against some of those same athletes whose posters had hung on my walls just a few years ago. It was surreal!

Neither team scored in the first half, and when the second half started, the novelty of where I was started to wear off. This was just a game like hundreds of others I'd played, and I tried to stay present and in the moment and ready for whatever the match brought. Around the fifty-nine-minute mark, the ball went out of play, and the Red Stars had a corner kick to restart the game. A fellow rookie, Vanessa DiBernardo, took the kick, and the ball was suddenly in the middle of a swarm of players from both sides right in front of the other team's goal.

You don't really have time to make conscious decisions in moments like that—you just hope your training and instincts kick in when it counts. Suddenly I was in front of the ball with a clear shot into the goal. I launched myself forward and felt my head con-

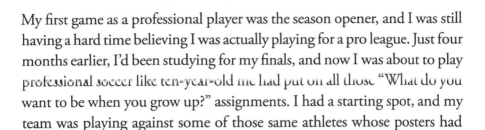

Making sacrifices is still a necessary part of my life.

nect. The next second, the ball was on the ground two feet over the goal line, and I was screaming and running toward my teammates, who were screaming and running toward me.

In the moment, I wasn't thinking *Wow, I just scored the first point of the season in a professional soccer match*—it was just a great moment in the game I loved, a victory I shared with my team, and something I was proud to have been a part of. The hope of moments like that was why I'd made the sacrifices I had, and I knew I would make those same hard choices all over again.

Making sacrifices is still a necessary part of my life. Since my husband and I are both professional athletes, we spend we spend a lot of time apart, which can be really hard. I live across the country from most of my family, so I don't see them very often, and I miss a lot of holidays and celebrations because of my travel schedule, just like in high school. But following the dreams God put in my heart and getting to use the talent He gave me is worth making some sacrifices for, and I plan to keep doing that as long as He lets me.

9

HARD WORK

It would be impossible to count exactly how many soccer games I've played in my life, but it's definitely more than a thousand. That sounds like a big number until you think about how many hours of practice and training each one of those games represents—now that's a *really* big number! Everyone knows you have to work hard in order to become good at something—teachers, parents, and coaches are always saying it. And it makes sense that to get really good, you have to work really hard.

I think we hear this a lot, but the reality of what hard work actually looks like on a daily basis can be a little tougher to understand. Maybe your idea of hard work is something physically challenging—something that makes you sweat, like yard work or lifting weights. Maybe you think of hard work as something with a high degree of difficulty, like complex math homework or learning an advanced piece of music on an instrument. Or you might associate hard work with a certain length of time—working a twelve-hour shift or spending a year writing a book.

All of these are great examples of work that is hard, but I think "hard work" as a concept is bigger than any one example. It's a combination of habits, attitude, and effort that is done to achieve a goal. Hard work has looked different at various times in my life, but it is without question one of the biggest factors in how I became the player I am today.

INSPIRING EXAMPLES

The best way to learn what hard work looks like is to watch people who already know how to do it. For me, those people were my parents. As far back as I can remember, they had the attitude that work done well has value and is something to be proud of. Growing up, I'd wake myself up for school because my parents were already at work. After school, I'd ride the bus home, and Melanie and I would get ready for soccer practice on our own because Mom and Dad were still at work. Mom would rush home just in time to pick us up, and then she'd spend the whole evening at practice with us before driving us home so we could fall into bed and do it all again the next day.

> My sister and I inherited a lot of our parents' work ethic from witnessing the matter-of-fact, uncomplaining approach they had to completing tasks.

I think my sister and I inherited a lot of our parents' work ethic from witnessing the matter-of-fact, uncomplaining approach they had to completing tasks. If something needed to be done, that's the way it was, so everybody just buckled down and made it happen. Getting to see firsthand that attitude toward hard work meant that I developed a strong sense of gratitude for all the opportunities my parents gave me. I never wanted to take the equipment and chances I had for granted or waste any extra training they paid for because I knew how hard they worked to give me those things. As I got older, I realized I'd also had a head start in learning how to work hard and work well toward a goal.

A lot of my soccer habits were formed almost without my recognizing it. I loved the game so much, and my early coaches were so great at making all the skills practice fun, that I would spend hours "working" without it feeling like work at all. When I started making the connection between the drills I loved doing and the reality that those things were actually "work," I was pretty excited. If I had to work to get better, like everyone said, that wasn't going to be a problem—work was fun! Of course, as I got older and the work got harder, it definitely was not always fun, but the habit had already been formed.

PLAYING UP

Once I made the connection between working and improving, I always asked my coaches if I could do extra work. I wanted to do whatever I could and as much as I could to get better. At the end of my first year playing for my first club, the coaches told my parents they wanted me to "play up" a year, which meant I would play on a team of girls who were a year older than I was. My parents let me make the decision.

"It's up to you, Julie," Dad said. "The girls are going to be bigger than you are, and they'll probably be better—at least as first—because they have a whole extra year of experience."

"The coach thinks you can do it, and we agree," said Mom, "but if you want to stick with your age group, that's okay."

I looked at the chance to play with the older team as a challenge. I knew I'd have to try my hardest to keep up, but it was fun to have to rise to the level of those older, stronger, faster girls. Going from a team where I was one of the better players to a team where most players were better than me was a great motivator to hit those drills and conditioning exercises even harder. Even when the work wasn't always fun, I was forming the habit of working hard because I saw what I could gain from it.

BUILDING CONFIDENCE

I've also found that putting in a lot of practice, especially when it involves repetition, is a great way to grow your confidence. When I feel really prepared for something, I am confident in myself. The people who are most nervous on the day of a test are usually those who didn't study. If you put in the work and spend the time, not only do you end up a better player than you started out, but you have more peace of mind and a positive outlook going into a game knowing you did everything in your power to prepare.

> It was fun to have to rise to the level of those older, stronger, faster girls.

This also makes losses sting a lot less. It's still never fun to lose, but if you can honestly say you did everything you could to prepare and worked as hard as you could during the game, it makes it easier to accept knowing you don't have any reason to be frustrated with yourself.

MANAGING TIME WELL

Don't get me wrong, forming good work habits is a process, and I definitely wasn't some perfect kid who had everything figured out! One skill that's especially important to develop is how to manage your time well. Time management is particularly important as a pro athlete because you're expected to do a lot of training and conditioning on your own. It took me longer to learn how to use my time well and plan ahead.

When I was around eleven or twelve years old, I went through a really bad procrastination stage. I don't know whether it was the more difficult projects I was assigned in school or that I was more interested in my social life than my homework, but again and again, I would wait until the last second to start assignments, and then they'd never come out like I wanted them to. Especially if the assignment involved a poster. If I had to make a poster, I would mentally block that project out until the last possible second.

"I HAVE PLENTY OF TIME"

In sixth grade, my teacher announced that the class was going to create a wax museum. Each student would select someone from a list she'd made of important people from history, research that person's life, write a biography, and create an exhibit (including a poster, of course) for the museum. The fun part was that we would stand in for the wax figures, meaning we would get to dress up as the person we picked. (Maybe it's just me, but I thought assignments where you got to dress up were the *best*.) I chose Eleanor Roosevelt. I thought of the presidents and their wives as the closest thing the U.S. had to royalty, so to sixth-grade me, a first lady was the coolest person I could dress up as.

I was *so* excited about the project the day it was assigned. My friends and I talked about it all the way home, and I was making elaborate plans in my head about what I'd wear, and the props I'd use, and cool things I could add to my exhibit. I started working on the project that same evening after school, but I quickly ran out of fun things to do—like think of costume ideas—and

> Time management is particularly important as a pro athlete because you're expected to do a lot of training and conditioning on your own.

needed to start the actual research. *No problem*, I thought. *It's not due for three weeks. I have plenty of time.* You can probably guess where this is going. Three weeks seemed like tons of time, and I kept putting it off.

Three weeks later, my mom was going through the handouts and permission slips in my backpack and called me into the kitchen.

"Julie, what's this reminder from your teacher about?" She was holding up a slip of paper that said "Don't Forget, Wax Museum This Thursday!" This was Tuesday night. My stomach dropped. *How has it been three weeks already?* I thought in a panic. My mom was reading the rest of the slip.

"A poster? A biography? An outfit? Have you done any of this?"

I slowly shook my head.

My mom and I stayed up all night Wednesday to get it done—me frantically writing the biography, Mom gluing pictures to the poster board and trying to scrounge up an Eleanor Roosevelt costume. Poor Mom was so tired at work the next day! We finished it, and it turned out pretty good, but I would have enjoyed the wax museum a lot more if I hadn't been about to fall asleep the whole time! I don't think I procrastinated again for a long time.

PLANNING VERSUS STRESSING

It's a funny story now, but the stress of those moments when you realize you've wasted your time is real. To avoid that stress, I became a huge planner. I plan out as much of my week in advance as I can and make a list of realistic goals for each day. I love checking those things off the list so I can see the progress I'm making. It helps me feel productive, which keeps me motivated to keep getting things done. This system has helped me a ton, keeping me from being stressed out by deadlines or long to-do lists.

I think keeping track of their own schedules and task lists is a habit that every young person should form. It helps you develop a sense of responsibility for your work that you're really going to need later. If you leave all that up to your mom or dad to handle for you, when you get to college, you're going to have a hard time adjusting to doing that all on your own. It's much better to do it now while you have your parents as a safety net if you make a mistake and while your teachers are more willing to forgive you if you make a poor decision.

PLATEAUS

As you get older and your goals get bigger, you'll find yourself having to adjust your definition of hard work. In fitness, there's a name for the phenomenon of working just as hard as you ever have but ceasing to make progress. It's called a "plateau," and it means your body isn't going to get any stronger or faster as long as you keep doing the same thing. If you want to keep improving, you have to change up your workout, add some intensity, switch out some of the moves. It doesn't just refer to your physical progress either—you can hit a mental plateau where you're stuck in the same thought patterns and attitudes.

> I plan out as much of my week in advance as I can and make a list of realistic goals for each day.

In August 2014, I joined the Women's National Team for a training camp that would decide who would play in the qualifying tournament for the World Cup. I worked my rear off at that camp—or at least, I told myself I did—but I fell just short of making the roster for the qualifying team. I was heartbroken when the coach told me I was close but just wasn't ready, but I knew she was right. Even though I had worked as hard as I could, I had failed, and that was hard to accept. When I got put on the team as an alternate after Crystal Dunn was injured, I knew I didn't deserve it. The others were just better and readier than I was, but I was grateful for the chance to be an alternate and determined to rise to my teammates' level.

NO HOLDING BACK

Over the next six months, I changed everything about my training. I drilled even the simplest skills over and over, breaking them down to the fundamental level and working each component separately. I put myself through such intense workouts, I sometimes got sick afterward because I had pushed myself so hard. I also realized that I'd been playing with the wrong attitude. I was waiting to be invited onto that world stage—I'd been playing pro soccer for seven months, but I was playing like a "new kid," like I needed to wait my turn to show what I could do rather than just going for it with all I had. I was done holding back, and that attitude shift helped me get to the level of working and training I needed to make the starting roster.

> I drilled even the simplest skills over and over, breaking them down to the fundamental level and working each component separately.

That's the way my relationship with hard work has gone my whole life: As I set each new, bigger goal, I found just enough motivation to get me to the next level of work needed to reach it. Today, those same habits I formed when I was just starting help keep me on track with the training schedule I maintain as a professional athlete, and now it's just my lifestyle.

I like to train in the morning because I find I feel better and make better food decisions the rest of the day if I do. This habit has turned me into a morning person, so now I love getting up early and having my coffee before I train. A typical in-season workout for me starts with a field/running routine before a weightlifting session. Every fifth day I take off from the normal routine. If I feel really good, I'll use that as my yoga day, but if my body needs some extra TLC, I'll take a complete rest day. In the off season, I ramp up the length and intensity of my training sessions to stay in shape because I'm not playing or practicing as much.

"I MADE THE ROSTER!"

I can't talk about hard work without talking about the payoff, because there will definitely be times when the skill feels too difficult, when the workout feels like it will never end, or you're sure you can't do one more push-up. In those moments, memories of the rewards of your work can help you find the strength to keep going.

One of the most exciting moments in my life happened after that period of intense training to try to make the World Cup roster. It was April 2015, and I was driving to Chicago from Philadelphia with my sister. I get way too bored on long drives by myself, so Melanie makes this trip with me. We have a blast, talking and telling funny stories while she does most of the driving. I don't get to see her a lot, so this has become a fun thing for us to do together a couple times a year.

> Memories of the rewards of your work can help you find the strength to keep going.

We were probably only about forty-five minutes outside of Philadelphia, playing cheesy music too loud, when my phone rang. The display read "Jill Ellis," the head coach of the Women's National Team. Without saying anything, I showed it to my sister, who had glanced over to see why I had stopped singing along. Instantly, she turned off the radio and I hit "Answer," my heart racing.

"Julie, hi, it's Jill. Just calling to congratulate you. You made the twenty-three for the World Cup this summer."

I honestly don't remember what I said next. It was a short call, and I think I stammered out some kind of "Thank you" and probably "See you soon," but my brain was having trouble keeping up with what I'd just heard. I hung up, and the car was quiet for a second—before Melanie couldn't stand it anymore.

"Well?" she demanded, looking between me and the road, trying to read my facial expression.

"I made the twenty-three."

I don't remember us screaming or crying, though maybe we did. All I remember is that we were both just so, so happy. We called Zach and Mom and Dad right away and repeated the good news, and my excitement and happiness grew every time I got to say "I made the roster." The rest of that long drive was a celebration of a dream took many years and a lot of hard work to come true.

10

BEING
COACHABLE

What steps would you to take to learn a new skill? For example, if you wanted to learn to swim, would you just throw yourself into the deep end of a pool and hope you figured it out on your own? Of course not! Would you try to learn from a book or a video? Maybe, but that would leave a lot of room for confusion or mistakes, and a book can't answer questions or give you feedback. No, the best way to learn how to do something or to get better at something is to be guided by someone who already knows how to do it and does it well. In soccer, of course, that person is the coach!

I am extremely blessed to be able to say I have had nothing but fabulous coaches my whole life. I mean, my first coach was my dad, so the bar was set pretty high for everyone who came after him, but from the rec league, to my youth club career, to college, to my pro teams, I have had one amazing coach after another. Of course, their influence in making me into the player I am today was huge, but I think it's

> I am extremely blessed to be able to say I have had nothing but fabulous coaches my whole life.

important for young players to know there wasn't anything magical about those coaches that led to my becoming a professional.

There are thousands of great coaches working all over the country right now, offering great advice and teaching valuable things about the game, yet only a fraction of the players they're coaching will ever turn pro. Why is that? It's not because those players didn't have great coaches. I think the biggest reason why good players don't become great players is not that they didn't have great coaches but that they weren't good at being coached.

LEARNING TO BE GOOD AT BEING COACHED

Being coachable means you have the kind of attitude and ability needed to both listen to and apply the instruction your coaches give you, and whether you're an athlete or not, it's one of the most important qualities you can have in life. You can hire the best coaches in the world to be your personal training squad, but if you aren't coachable, you're never going to be a great player. No matter how much you work with them, if you don't know how to take criticism and advice humbly and how to accept help from people who are wiser and more talented than you, you might as well quit, because that team of fabulous coaches isn't going to have the slightest effect on you.

Being coachable is a skill you can develop like any other, and because it's so important, it's one you should cultivate as early as you can. There are many ways you can mold yourself into a coachable player—habits you can form, attitudes you can practice, and ways to change your perspective to make it easier to learn all you can from the experts in your life.

ASK FOR HELP

I learned the most important lesson about being coachable early in my career, and if I hadn't, I'm confident there wouldn't have been a "later" in my career! This lesson sounds simple, but for twelve-year-old me, it felt like the hardest thing in the world: Ask for help when you need it.

Now, it was nothing new to me to need help. In school, I was better at some subjects than others, like anyone, but it didn't bother me too much when I found myself struggling—probably because from the time Melanie and I started school, our parents taught us to look at education as a service that existed to help us. That attitude really helped take any embarrassment or shame out of asking my parents or my teachers for support. When something was giving me trouble, I didn't take it personally—I let someone help me.

> Being coachable is a skill you can develop like any other, and because it's so important, it's one you should cultivate as early as you can.

With soccer, however, it was a different story. Soccer was something I was already good at and was proud of my abilities in, so it was extra hard for me to handle when I had trouble with a certain skill or trick. *But this is my thing! I'm not supposed to have trouble with this*, I would think stubbornly, and I'd keep trying to figure it out on my own, which would only make me more frustrated.

A LESSON FROM THE LIGHT POST

When I was about twelve, I was having a hard time juggling. We had a drill where we had to juggle down to a light post and back, and I'd been trying for a couple of weeks and was still struggling to do it. My default response when I wasn't able to do something was to get mad and shut down, and the more I tried and failed, the madder I got.

> Some of the best advice I have to give, whether you're an athlete or not, is that if you're having a hard time with something, know you are *not* alone!

Finally, my mom, seeing how frustrated I was, casually asked, "Why don't you ask the coach if you can spend some extra time working on that juggling drill?" Maybe it was the way she phrased it, making it sound like a bonus to get to spend more time working on something, but I agreed to ask the coach to work with me. And wouldn't you know, after I spent that time getting help, I got the hang of it no problem.

YOU AREN'T ALONE

After that, I'd ask my coach for more time or extra help whenever I was struggling with a skill. After I saw how much easier things were when I accepted help from others, I wondered why I wasted so much time being frustrated on my own.

Some of the best advice I have to give, whether you're an athlete or not, is that if you're having a hard time with something, know you are *not* alone! There are so many people in your life—your teachers, your coaches, and your family—who want to support you. Learning to be vulnerable, or understanding your weaknesses and being willing to ask for help, is one of the best ways you can grow as a person.

TRUST AND RESPECT

A big factor in how well you will respond to your coaches is whether you really respect and trust them. You can be polite and respectful in your words toward them, but if you don't really believe they know what they're talking about and accept their judgment, you're not going to get all you could out of their training and advice. I respected my coaches so much that I never wanted to let them down. I recognized that they knew a lot more and had a lot more experience than I did, so if I did something wrong, it never occurred to me to blame them—I was just disappointed in myself for not doing better after they'd tried to teach me so much.

When you decide you really trust your coach to do what's best for you and your team, you have to be willing to accept all his decisions, even when you don't agree with them. I remember getting benched once during a game. I wasn't performing well, and my coach took me out. In that moment, I definitely didn't agree with his decision, and I did not respond well. I didn't complain to my coach because that would have been rude, but I spent the rest of the game upset and fuming on the sidelines. I wasn't paying attention to what was going on out on the field and wasn't learning anything because I was so busy thinking about how unfair it was that I'd been taken out of the game.

> I respected my coaches so much that I never wanted to let them down.

After the game, I was still upset, and I ran to my mom for some sympathy. She let me vent a little bit, but in the car on the way home, she asked me a question that made me rethink my attitude.

"Julie, do you trust your coach?"

I answered right away. "Well, yeah, but—"

She stopped me. "But nothing. Think about it—do you believe that your coach wants what's best for you? And what's best for the team?"

I thought a little longer before answering this time. "Yes," I said, still glum.

She nodded. "I thought so. You've learned a lot from him and played some really great games for him. If you believe he's worth learning from when it's fun and when you're winning, you have to continue to respect him even when you don't like a decision he makes."

> If I really wanted to benefit from everything my coach had to offer, I had to respect him not just with my words but by trusting his decisions.

"But I didn't say anything rude to him!" I protested.

Mom shook her head. "No, but being polite isn't the same thing as being respectful. If you'd respected his decision, you would still have been bummed, but instead of questioning his judgment, you would be looking for what he wanted you to learn from this." I thought about that as she continued, "You either trust him or you don't, and if you do, that means you accept all his calls and look for the lessons you can learn from them because you know he's doing what's best for you and the team."

That conversation with my mom really helped me evaluate my attitude toward my coach and see that if I really wanted to benefit from everything he had to offer, I had to respect him not just with my words but by trusting his decisions.

MAINTAINING A COACHABLE ATTITUDE

It also helped me develop a coachable attitude when I would see players who were definitely *not* bringing a teachable spirit to the field. I almost never saw this from one of my teammates because the Sereno players had to try out for their spots every year, and the coaches selected players who showed they were eager to learn and had good attitudes. If you were playing for Sereno, you knew you were getting a lot of great opportunities as part of that club, and none of the girls wanted to jeopardize their place with bad behavior.

Other teams, however, were sometimes a very different story. Over the years, I saw players roll their eyes or ignore a coach when she gave them a suggestion or just shut down and stop trying in the middle of a game because they were so upset by a coach's correction. I even saw a few players yelling at their coaches, which my teammates and I were shocked by.

I also saw firsthand how an inability to take direction from your coach also hurts your team. It was during a state cup game. We were up 1–0, and I could tell from the way an opposing player stomped off the field that this girl was really frustrated. During a time-out, her coach was trying to tell her something—probably to encourage her because they were only down by one point and there was still a half hour left in the game—but when she came back onto the field, you could tell she hadn't heard a word he'd said.

She had that shut-down, I-don't-care-anymore look on her face, as did several of her teammates, and that's when my team knew we were going to win that state championship. The other team could have easily salvaged the game, but that give-up attitude kept spreading, and no matter how their coach tried to motivate them, they responded with frustration.

We tried to win as graciously as possible, but all the time I was thinking, *Here*

> That one player's attitude set the tone for the rest of the team.

you have a coach taking the time to try to help you—why aren't you listening to him? That one player's attitude set the tone for the rest of the team. Her teammates could have tried to cheer her on, but they saw her reaction to the coach and thought she was a lost cause. Seeing that hard-to-coach attitude and its impact on an entire team made me realize I never wanted to be that type of player.

We all have bad days and make mistakes, and chances are the high stakes of the state championship pushed that player to make some bad choices, but the fact that I still remember being shocked by how she responded to her coach reinforces my resolve: I don't want to be remembered as the player who couldn't take feedback from her coach with maturity and grace.

A GOOD FIT

I can say a lot about the importance of having a good attitude and trusting your coach, but it's also essential to point out that a big part of a player's success in doing those things depends on how good a fit her coach is for her goals and her needs. Don't get me wrong—every coach has something he can teach you. It's important to try to get along with and learn from all kinds of people, but the reality is that in life, you'll meet people you respond better to or "click with" more than others. Sometimes that has to do with personalities or communication styles, but if you're going to commit to learning from and abiding by the decisions of a coach, make sure that person's vision and goals for you match your own.

> The coaches were welcoming and enthusiastic, and it felt like they were interested in me as a person—not just my statistics.

When you get to your last two years of high school, get ready for a lot of decision-making! Whether you're planning to go to college, start a career, or pursue other types of education, you'll need to put a lot of thought into what's next. At the end of my sophomore year, I had lots of things to consider as I looked at my options for playing soccer in college. I'd visited ten different schools before I got the letter from Santa Clara. I was waiting for something in my heart to tell me that a certain school was *the* school, and every time I visited a new campus, I thought, *Maybe this will be it!*

Again and again, though, I would get to a school and feel disappointed. I liked most of them just fine, but I was bummed because I still hadn't felt that conviction that I'd found a really good match. When I went to Santa Clara, it felt like home, and the coaches there were a big part of that. They were welcoming and enthusiastic, and it felt like they were interested in me as a person—not just my statistics.

The Santa Clara coaches already knew me well as a player and showed a personal interest in me, telling me what they liked about me as an athlete or what they'd noticed when they'd watched me at tournaments or on game film. I felt like they had my best interests at heart when they talked about what my future at Santa Clara would look like. It was like they knew and valued me for me. That conviction made it easy to put myself under their direction and trust them with the next few vital years of my training and career.

CRITICISM CAN HELP

The last big piece of being coachable is maybe the hardest one: You have to learn how to take criticism. Especially if you want to keep getting better at something, you're going to have to listen to some things you'd rather not hear about yourself and your weaknesses. It's not always fun, but it's the only way to improve and move forward.

People who can't listen to criticism from those who are best equipped

> Correction and criticism are just opportunities to get better.

to offer it will stop making progress. I was lucky to grow up in an environment where feedback was given constantly, so I got used to receiving it early on, but it was still hard to hear sometimes. When you're getting correction in an activity you love so much and are trying so hard at, it can be difficult not to take it personally. But you should always try to remind yourself that correction and criticism are just opportunities to get better.

Throughout your life, your ability to respond well to the people with more experience and knowledge than you will play a big part in your success. So when you know you have a good coach—whether that's a teacher, a parent, or your actual coach—make the most of it. Learn all you can from these people and treat them like partners in your journey to reach your goals. They can definitely help you get there if you let them.

11

TEAMWORK

When I was two, my family moved into a brand-new neighborhood. Just about every family moving in had young children, and as a result, I grew up in a close-knit community with tons of kids within a five- or six-year age range. Some of my earliest memories are of playing kickball, tag, and soccer with my neighbors in our cul-de-sac.

With no ref and no scoreboard, these games gave me my first taste of the thrill of a group of people getting together to do something more fun than anything any of them could have done by themselves. I realize now that when I started playing sports for real, I was looking for something that would match the excitement of those earliest games with my first "team."

The fact that soccer is a team sport has always been one of my absolute favorite things about the game. For me, sports where you're competing by yourself just aren't as fun or as interesting as activities where a group of individuals pools their talents and works as a unit to carry out a strategy or complete a play. It's hard learning to read one another and react collectively

> I've been blessed to be part of incredible teams my whole life, and the lessons they've taught me and the experiences we've shared are some of the greatest gifts the game of soccer has given me.

in the moment, but for me, that's what makes soccer *so cool*! The excitement of that many people being in the right places at the right time to successfully maneuver one little soccer ball across a massive field covered in live, intelligent obstacles—there's nothing like it.

For obvious reasons, a ton of your training as a soccer player has to do with teamwork. You can do as much juggling, shooting, and dribbling practice on your own as you want, but if you don't understand the formations and strategies that will be used on the field, or if you don't understand the role of the different players and positions, you're never going to have much success in a game. A strong team can pick off a strong player working on her own every time. I've been blessed to be part of incredible teams my whole life, and the lessons they've taught me and the experiences we've shared are some of the greatest gifts the game of soccer has given me.

A SHARED GOAL

Every player on a soccer team has at least one goal in common with all her teammates: Score enough points to win the game. Depending on the level of the team, the players might have other individual goals. On a recreational team, one player might want to play in college, another might only be playing to keep busy until swim season starts, and yet another might play three sports and two instruments and plays soccer because she enjoys it. As you move to a school or club team, however, more of the players are going to be serious about the sport. They will share bigger goals, like winning tournaments, playing in college, or even going pro. That doesn't mean the players have to give up the other things they enjoy, but soccer becomes a bigger priority, and they share that with their teammates.

When I made the move to my first soccer club from a casual rec league, I was suddenly surrounded by players who were a lot more like me, who loved soccer and loved to compete. It just makes sense that a team of more like-minded players would have more success, both because the individual members are more motivated and are putting in more work to better themselves and because they feel more responsibility toward their team when everyone wants to win.

> My journey to state with that team had shown me how much more a win means when your whole team is invested in it— when you know you did it together and couldn't have done it any other way.

CHAMPIONSHIP TEAMWORK

That unity was one of the things that got us all the way to the state championship the year I was twelve. It was everyone's first time playing at state, so our excitement level was through the roof. And as if it wasn't cool enough to be competing for the state cup, the winners would get to play at regionals in *Hawaii*. You can imagine how psyched we were! I don't remember ever wanting to win a game as badly as I did that state championship.

My journey to state with that team had shown me how much more a win means when your whole team is invested in it—when you know you did it together and couldn't have done it any other way. You feel prouder of your successes because you know they helped your team get closer to the win, and you want the win not for yourself but for the team.

The game was tied near the end of the first half. Everyone's focus was super sharp, and we were all staying in the moment, formations scattering and reforming all down the field as we waited for one of those perfect intersections of players, goal, and ball. I don't even remember recognizing that moment with any extra excitement when it came. All I know is that suddenly, I was at midfield with the ball. I don't remember looking at the goal—I just felt the need to shoot. I was just barely past the half line, so it didn't really make sense to shoot, but I did it anyway without hesitating, and it went in.

> You can love to win and still win with grace.

I'd scored plenty of goals in my life before that one and won plenty of games, but the elation I felt was on another level from my previous experiences. It was like waking up on Christmas morning. That goal ended up being the game winner, and I had never been so ecstatic. I'd helped my team win the state cup and a trip to Hawaii, and I was thrilled to be able to do that for my teammates.

WINNING WITH GRACE

I still feel that excitement of winning, even many years and many wins later. I think it's a common misunderstanding that there's something wrong with loving to win—a love of winning has somehow gotten associated with being a sore winner, and that's not always the case. You can love to win and still win with grace.

Sure, you have to love the game apart from the victory or you'll never make it through the tedium of practice and the disappointment of losses. But to enjoy the competition of a well-matched, fair game; to love the excitement of being successful in that game; and then to share that success with your teammates—like I said, Christmas morning. I don't think there's anything wrong with feeling that way as long as you're not obsessing over winning or measuring your worth as a person by whether you win or lose.

SHARING THE UPS AND DOWNS

Not all the lessons you learn with or from your team are as fun and fulfilling as what it feels like to win together. No matter how good your team is, you will experience defeat on the field. You'll experience the normal ups and downs of life, and sharing all this with your team brings you even closer together than the victories.

One of my biggest "lows" was when I hurt my back in high school and thought I was going to have to stop playing. That was the hardest thing I could imagine going through at the time, and throughout that injury, my team was there for whatever I needed, always trying to put a smile on my face and lift my spirits.

> You'll experience the normal ups and downs of life, and sharing all this with your team brings you even closer together than the victories.

When I thought I might have to give up on my soccer dreams, it would have been easy to give in to that fear and negativity, but my team surrounded me with support and with encouragement that kept me hopeful.

GROWING UP TOGETHER

Your teammates become your support system for a lot more than just soccer-related problems, especially when you're young. Between the training, the games, and the travel, my teammates and I basically grew up together. From braces, to crushes, to playground drama, everything seemed a little easier and a little less scary because we were going through it as a group, and we always had each other's backs.

One of the things I've always thought is especially cool about sports is the way they can create an instant bond between people who have nothing else in common. Once when I was fourteen, and again when I was seventeen, I got invited to youth camps sponsored by U.S. Soccer. These camps were a way for U.S. Soccer to identify and develop some of the best players in an age group in the country, and I was excited to be invited, but it was an adjustment not to have my regular team around me.

> Our love for the game and our drive to improve united us, and I found myself able to be really vulnerable and real with my camp teammates.

I was surprised by how quickly the other campers and I felt like a team even though we'd only been playing together for a few days. I wanted to make a good impression and play my best at those camps, so if I had a bad day or made a mistake, it was really frustrating, but these girls who I'd just met were there to keep my mind off it or motivate me to do better, whichever I needed.

You might have expected that kind of environment to be a little more cutthroat—that all of those highly ambitious, competitive girls would be likely to view each other as the competition in an environment where we all wanted to be noticed. But our love for the game and our drive to improve united us, and I found myself able to be really vulnerable and real with my camp teammates.

SETTING AN EXAMPLE

It's no secret that the people you associate with have a direct impact on your attitude, your behavior, and the kind of person you become. That's why it's so important to surround yourself with positive people who are setting a good example. If your teammates complain, disrespect their coaches, or have negative attitudes, that's going to have a lousy effect on your own character.

When I would witness bad behavior from a player on an opposing team—whether that was yelling at her coach, arguing with a ref, or playing dirty—my first reaction was usually pity that her team wasn't doing more to help her. To my mind, being a good teammate meant you intervened with compassion when you saw a teammate with an attitude that was self-destructive or whose actions could hurt the team. You can't make someone behave a certain way, but you can set a good example and try to help her get past those negative behaviors or attitudes.

WHAT'S BEST FOR THE TEAM . . .

One of the hardest things to learn about teamwork is how to want what's best for your team even when it might not be best for you. Every player on the sidelines wants to be out on the field, but the reality is that sometimes your role in the game is to cheer your team on from the bench. It can be hard to accept that another player might do more for the game than you can, but when your coach makes that call, you have to respect it.

The same goes for when you're the one getting criticism from your coach. Especially when you're younger, you can feel self-conscious when you're getting correction, and that can feel like negative attention. Watching my teammates respond to correction was a big help to me in adjusting my perspective because I could see how a player improved when she listened to and applied the feedback she was given. It became natural to want that feedback myself and to look at it as a chance to become a better player. I'm grateful to have been on a team with girls who were mature enough to set that example for me.

. . . AND WHAT'S BEST FOR YOU

Even if you don't play a sport, the principles of working together and supporting each other are important lessons to learn for life, even if your "team" is just the people who are closest to you. Most friendships are formed between people with similar values and likes, so it makes sense that a lot of your closest friends will come from your sports team, your dance class, your theater group, or whatever activity you're passionate about. When you're on a team like that, you can't help but end up closer as you go through different phases of life together.

My closest circle of friends has taught me that one of the most valuable traits in a teammate, whether in your sports team or your life "team," is that she wants what's best for you. I've been blessed with amazing friends who truly understood about soccer either because they play or played in the past themselves or because they truly care about *me* and know what an important part of my life it is.

> Working together and supporting each other are important lessons to learn for life, even if your "team" is just the people who are closest to you.

It can be easy for me to feel guilty for my busy schedule, but my friends know what my goals are and unselfishly want those same goals for me, even though it means they don't get to spend very much time with me.

These are the friends who make time for me around my crazy schedule, who figure out time zones and do math before they call or text me because I travel so much, and who drop what they are doing and help anytime I need them. It's not fair on their end, but they love me enough to want me to be able to chase my professional dreams, and I am so, so grateful to them and to God for putting them in my life.

MY CLOSEST TEAMMATE

My closest teammate these days is my husband, Zach. I didn't really have serious boyfriends growing up. At the age when other girls want boyfriends, my life was all soccer, all the time. It was hard because while I wanted to spend time on "normal" high school experiences and make those classic memories, I also had big dreams and goals I wasn't willing to compromise, so I felt like I couldn't give time to a relationship yet.

When I got to college, I was even more focused on soccer, so dating was never anything serious as much as it was just having fun and hanging out with good friends. When I met Zach, I was struck by how alike we were in that we were both serious college players on the point of (hopefully) beginning our pro careers. Being with someone with similar aspirations was freeing. I'd always felt like I had to apologize to people for my ambition—like I should feel guilty for making my goals a priority—but Zach understood and had the same drive, and we both really felt seen.

It's funny to think he was waiting for me in the future while I was growing up worrying that I wasn't going to have a relationship like that for a long time, if ever, because of my goals. Having a teammate who shares and supports my goals and whom I can support in return is amazing, and it doesn't hurt that he's pretty cute too!

BE KIND TO YOURSELF

A lot of times when coaches talk about teamwork, I think what players hear is that the team is more important than the individual. After all, we've all heard the phrase "There's no 'I' in team," but I've learned it's also essential that you work on and take care of yourself as an individual.

I find it as important to work on your friendship with yourself as it is to work on your relationships with your teammates. You have to be on a team with yourself every game you ever play, so you better like yourself and treat yourself well. It can be just as damaging to have a bad relationship with yourself as it is to have a bad relationship with another player or a coach.

You have to trust yourself to make good decisions and go with your instincts. Players who doubt themselves or feel inferior freeze up or hang back in the big moments of the game, which hurts everyone on their team. To be a good friend to yourself, you have to take care of your health, own your skills and what you bring to the field, and take time for personal growth.

> I find it as important to work on your friendship with yourself as it is to work on your relationships with your teammates.

Yes, teamwork sometimes means the individual takes a backseat to what's best for the team, but it doesn't mean "be quiet and get along." I always remind myself that living to please people is a bad way to live. You're never going to be able to please everyone, and if you try, you're likely to end up compromising in ways you'll regret. Work on your weaknesses, yes, but then let that hard work be heard—own your strengths and recognize what you bring to that team!

12

FAMILY

think I've already mentioned my mom's maroon van she used to drive my sister and me to and from soccer practice. My mom nicknamed it the Cranberry, and I thought it was the dorkiest car in the world. The Cranberry had a decal in the back window, kind of like the stick-figure families you see everywhere. This sticker showed a van carrying a family just like ours—with a mom, a dad, and two girls—but where the wheels would be, the van had soccer balls, and across the side was the word "Taxi." It was *officially* a soccer-mom van, and my dad teased my mom about that sticker as long as she drove it.

That little sticker family in the soccer van was the perfect picture of my family when I was growing up. Once Melanie and I decided we loved soccer and wanted to play seriously, the whole family got on board and pursued that goal together. For some families, sports or activities mean less time together, but for us, soccer was the reason we spent hours in the car together traveling all over the country, and it was our chance to show our support for each other—no matter what. My family was my first team and my earliest role models, and my relationships with them and the examples they set shaped me into the person I am today.

BEING THERE

I've already talked a lot about my parents and how they worked so hard and made so many sacrifices to give Melanie and me not just what we needed but many incredible extra opportunities. Yes, that hard work and sacrifice made an impression, and we were definitely grateful for it, but Mom and Dad poured into our lives in a meaningful way by actually being present in them as much as they possibly could.

After working all week, Dad could have felt like he'd already done his part in supporting our soccer playing and stayed at home for some well-earned rest. Instead, every Friday afternoon he climbed into the Cranberry with the rest of us as we headed off to the next tournament. Mom could have dropped us off at a game and gone to run some errands once in a while. Instead, she was on the sidelines watching and cheering like each game was the World Cup. Both parents would have been completely justified in demanding that we spend at least one Thanksgiving dinner at home instead of at Denny's because we were on the road for yet another tournament, but they never did (and we ate a lot of Thanksgiving dinners at Denny's).

> Mom and Dad poured into our lives in a meaningful way by actually being present in them as much as they possibly could.

Don't get me wrong—my parents were the final authority in the family, not the soccer schedule, but even though they didn't have to, they chose to be a part of all those games and practices and travel. They knew that with the demands of playing for an elite club, the only way we could still enjoy time together as a family was if they came along and got involved in whatever ways they could, whether that was running a fundraiser, driving a carpool, or simply cheering us on.

They definitely weren't hovering; they always let the coach be the coach, and they never interfered in a game or a practice, but they were present. When Melanie and I were playing in different games at the same time, Mom would watch one of us and Dad would watch the other, keeping each other updated via walkie-talkie, and then switch at halftime. The older I get, the more I see what a gift they gave us with their wholehearted, unselfish commitment to staying close as a family. It gave Melanie and me an unshakeable sense of confidence to see our parents be so intentional about making time with us a priority. No one else could have taught me so well what it truly means to support and cheer on your teammates.

LIFE WITH MY BIG SISTER

There's an old song you might have heard that's basically a duet between two people who are fighting over who's the best. "Anything you can do, I can do better," they keep challenging each other. That song pretty much summarizes the relationship between my sister and me growing up. We're really close now, but when we were younger, we lived in a constant state of competition. Melanie is only two years older than I am, and like most little sisters, I wanted nothing more than to be *just* like her—though I never would have admitted it. It drove me crazy that I couldn't

> Melanie is only two years older than me, and like most little sisters, I wanted nothing more than to be *just* like her.

catch up with her in either age or height, and I devoted the majority of my energy to trying to be as good as she was.

As much as I wanted to do the same things Melanie did, we were polar opposites in personality. Melanie was shy and introverted. I, on the other hand, never met a person I couldn't talk to. She was self-conscious and didn't like to draw attention to herself, while I loved being in the spotlight and didn't really care about what people thought.

FUN AND GAMES . . . MOST OF THE TIME

When I was in second grade, both Melanie and I got glasses. Truth be told, I didn't actually need them, but when I found out my sister was getting glasses, I suddenly had a lot more trouble with my vision.

I'm sure the eye doctor saw right through me, but he must have figured, *Hey, if the kid wants glasses so bad, let her have glasses.* The first day we were going to wear them to school, Melanie was scared. The change was sure to invite some attention, maybe even some jokes, and she was petrified at the thought of being called a geek. As for me, I couldn't wait to show mine off—and if someone had told me I looked like a geek, I probably would have thought that was hilarious.

My attitude was usually more lighthearted than my sister's. I just didn't take things as seriously as she did. In competition, Melanie was all about the win. I wanted to win, but I also wanted to have fun. I think that was a good combination for us; she pushed me to try harder, and I helped her take things less seriously. We loved that we always had someone to play with—and not just soccer. We spent hours making up ridiculous games in the backyard that were probably only fun because we were sisters.

That's not to say we didn't have our share of fights. I don't think two sisters can go through middle school and high school together and not have at least a few squabbles. I'd get in trouble with Melanie for wearing her clothes or using her hair products. She'd forbid me to touch her stuff, but I'd just wait to "borrow" her clothes until after she had left for school. She'd hide her conditioner so I couldn't use it, but I'd find it and use it anyway—okay, so she might have been justified in getting mad.

> She pushed me to try harder, and I helped her take things less seriously.

"THOSE JOHNSTON GIRLS!"

One of our worst fights is funny to remember now. One day in middle school, I had to stay after school to make up a test I'd missed the week before for a soccer tournament. Melanie could drive by this time, and I loved riding with her—probably a lot more than she loved having to give her little sister rides all the time. After my test, I called her to ask if she could come pick me up. And if I'm being honest, I probably *told* her to come get me more than I *asked* her. Since Mom and Dad made her drive me around so much, I might have acted a little too entitled to her taxi services, which is probably why the conversation went the way it did.

"I can't," she said when I'd "asked."

"What? Why not?" I demanded.

"I just can't. I'm out with friends."

"Come on, it's like a five-minute trip!" I begged.

"Ride the bus!" she shot back.

"The busses already left!"

"Well, I guess you're walking, then!" And she hung up.

The trip home was probably only a few miles, and it's not like I wasn't in good shape, but three miles in Arizona weather when you're furious feels like a lot more. With every step I took, I got madder and madder at Melanie. I thought about all the things I was going to tell Mom and Dad about how I had spent all my homework time walking home because she wouldn't come get me—and what if I'd gotten heatstroke? What if I'd been hit by a car, thank you very much? Then she'd be sorry!

Just as I was walking into our neighborhood, my sister pulled up in the car alongside me. Maybe she'd started to feel bad. Maybe (and I think this is more likely) she'd started to get nervous about what I'd tell Mom and Dad, but she rolled down the window and in a super friendly voice said, "Get in! I'll drive you home."

"Are you kidding?" I cried. "Half a block from home? Thanks for nothing!"

I started walking faster, and she continued to crawl along in the car next to me.

"Come on, get in the car," she pleaded.

"*No!*"

We walked/drove the rest of the way home like that, yelling back and forth at each other from the sidewalk and the car. If any of the neighbors saw us, they probably thought those Johnston girls were crazy.

Anyone with siblings can probably emphasize with that stubborn, ridiculous fight. I don't remember what happened when we got home, but there was probably a lot of mutual complaining about the other one to Mom and Dad, a slammed door or two, and then, after a little more grumbling, peace. When your sister is also your best friend, you eventually get tired of being mad at her and go back to (mostly) getting along.

> When your sister is also your best friend, you eventually get tired of being mad at her and go back to (mostly) getting along.

SISTER-FRIENDS

I feel like a sibling is the closest friend you can have. Regardless of whether you get along all the time (and I don't know *any* siblings who get along all the time), your siblings are in your life for good, and they share your same experiences and heritage. No one understands you better. I would get so mad at Melanie sometimes, but at the end of the day, we were best friends. I told her everything, and still do, and she was always there to help me navigate the trials of growing up with her big-sister wisdom—even after I grew six inches taller than her.

As we got older, we had our own friends from school and soccer, and of course sometimes we spent more time on those friendships than our relationship with each other, but that sibling connection was always there. When she went away to college, I missed her, but I was also excited to get my hands on the car once she left. Then as I went through senior year and my first years in college, that connection with my sister grew more important.

My other friends were all over the country at different colleges, heading in different life directions, and my relationship with my sister became more precious because I had the assurance of it being permanent. It gave me peace in a scary time to know Melanie would be a constant presence in my life. Ironically, even though we were far apart in distance, we got closer in college, and our relationship has continued to grow stronger—something I'm thankful for every day.

IT'S WHAT FAMILIES DO

I've also always been close with my extended family of aunts, uncles, cousins, second cousins, and grandparents. As far back as I can remember, everyone was always checking on everyone else, making sure we were all okay.

> My family never missed an opportunity to support one another, going to games, concerts, and performances.

My family never missed an opportunity to support one another, going to games, concerts, and performances whenever it was possible. I have a lot of cousins, so that was a lot of games and concerts and performances, but that was okay. Supporting each other was what family did, and that meant you invested your time. As a result, everyone felt known and loved, and that is still the truest definition of family I can think of.

Whether you realize it or not, the influence your family has on the kind of person you become is huge. Your family is your background—they're who you come from and who you belong to. Their experiences, stories, and values affect what you think is important and how you see yourself.

MY FAMILY AND MY COUNTRY

As an example, I grew up in a family that was very patriotic. They believed living in this country was a privilege, and they were proud to belong to it and proud of the people who served it. Our flag was always out on flag holidays, and we were that big family who wore coordinating patriotic shirts on the Fourth of July.

My grandpa served in the navy, and because of him, my family assigned a lot of importance to respecting and honoring the troops and veterans. My family taught and modeled gratitude toward those who had served our country, and so I grew up sharing that value.

When I was in second grade, my school put on a performance at the end of the year where every class did something like sing a song or perform a skit for the rest of the school and for our families. For our part of the program, my class sang "God Bless America," and my teacher told each student we could invite someone who had served or was serving in the military onstage to thank during the song.

I knew the perfect person—my grandpa. All my life, I had seen how my family respected and honored him for his service, and now I wanted to be part of that tradition. I was so excited to ask him, I called him about thirty seconds after I got home from school.

> My family taught and modeled gratitude toward those who had served our country, and so I grew up sharing that value.

The day of the program, Grandpa sat in the front row with all the other guests of honor, and I remember being so proud of him. After we finished the first half of the song, our guests came onto the stage, and one at a time, we met them at the microphone to say our thanks. The moment I thanked my grandpa in front of the whole school is one of my favorite memories because it made me feel connected to what was important to my family.

My family's emphasis on being grateful for this country and honoring the people who represent its best ideals make it an especially cool thing every time I get to play for the United States. The first game I played for the national team, I felt a sense of awe wearing the crest for the first time. It was such an honor to be representing my country and doing what I loved most.

Knowing my family's tradition of national pride, it made me love playing for the U.S. team even more. My "service" is nothing compared to what our servicemen and women do, but I'm happy if I can represent my country even in a small way by playing my absolute hardest on the international stage. Even now, after the World Cup and the Olympics, I still get goosebumps when we sing the national anthem and I realize I'm representing the country that means so much to my family.

I'm not saying you have to love everything your family loves or that they won't accept you if you don't have the same values and priorities as they do, but in my experience, discovering those connections to what you have in common gives you a special sense of belonging and of your place in your family. I am thankful for the ways my family has shaped me into the person I am and proud to belong to such an amazing group of people. I always encourage young athletes to invest in their families, their parents, and their siblings because those are the people whose support will follow you through all the wins and losses of your life.

> I still get goosebumps when we sing the national anthem and I realize I'm representing the country that means so much to my family.

13

A DREAM
COME TRUE

Vancouver, 2015, twenty-four hours before the World Cup Final. The stands at BC Place were empty—hundreds of rows of red seats waiting for the fifty-five thousand spectators who would pack the place at tomorrow's final. The U.S. team was having our last training session before the game the next day.

Each team got to train at the stadium the day before the game so we could get a feel for the space and the pitch. Because our schedule for the last month had been so crazy, the training was light—just enough to flex our muscles and test our speed a little—and I was feeling really good. Everything seemed to click; my body felt right, everyone was looking sharp, and my excitement for the next day was sky high. After our workout, most players headed back to the hotel for an early night, though no one slept very well.

THE DAY OF THE GAME

I woke up the next day still enjoying that sense of deep well-being. I checked my phone, responding to a few good-luck texts from friends back home, and made plans with Zach, then my boyfriend, to grab an early coffee. Along with my family, Zach had traveled to Vancouver for the final, and I was eager to see him before the game. I usually had to FaceTime him before my games, so having the chance to talk in person was amazing.

> I started to lock in like I do before every game—headphones in, music blaring, visualizing the match.

We didn't talk much about soccer. He kept my mind off the game by chatting about other stuff, and we walked around downtown Vancouver so I could get my legs moving until it was time for the team to head to the stadium. I kissed Zach good-bye, grabbed my stuff, and climbed on the bus with my teammates.

Once we got on the bus, I started to lock in like I do before every game—headphones in, music blaring, visualizing the match. As the bus got closer to the stadium, we started to see people standing outside, holding up homemade signs with our players' names on them. Since the game was being held so close to the U.S., tons of fans had made the trip, and seeing them lining the streets decked out in USA gear made me feel at home and at peace. The stadium came into view, and it looked immaculate. My mom and dad, Melanie, my grandma, several cousins, and Zach and his mom would all be watching from somewhere inside.

PREGAME

We got to our locker room, and I immediately started my pregame ritual of a shower to wake myself up before prayer with my teammates. Some people don't understand why athletes pray before games—like maybe God doesn't care about sports or has more important things to do than help people win a game. But God cares about everything we care about, and He's happy for us to ask Him for protection from injury, for sharp minds and strong bodies, and yes, for His help doing our best so we can win. Praying helps me put the game in God's hands and gives me a good perspective before the match starts.

> Praying helps me put the game in God's hands and gives me a good perspective before the match starts.

In what seemed like no time, we were leaving the locker room to warm up. Just like the day before, our rhythm on the field was spot on—every drill working like clockwork, everyone's shooting looking great. I didn't want to comment on it to anyone because I felt like that would jinx it, but I was in awe of our team, and now the seconds were speeding on toward the coin toss.

MINUTE FIFTEEN

We were up 3–0. The rhythm and energy of our warm-up kept gaining momentum, and again and again, our maneuvers played out like a dream, and the ball hit the back of the net. We were thrilled to be up by so much so early, but I knew we had to be locked in because in a game of that level, the tables can turn at any second.

Minute sixteen, we scored again, up by four!

Minute twenty-seven, Japan scored, and my heart broke. The girl I was stuck to scored because I overstepped. It happened in a split second, and I was so upset with myself, but I knew it would do more damage if I couldn't leave that moment in the past and move on mentally. *It's okay, you're fine*, I told myself fiercely. *Stay in the game, stay in the moment, keep going!* We were still up, it wasn't the end of the world—and I shook it off and dove back into the game.

THIRTY MINUTES TO GO

Every second of the game was a battle. With thirty minutes to go, we were up 5–2, and now we were playing a little more defensively—we didn't want to give up goals. Twenty minutes to go, and we were all in a frenzy. Our one objective was to run out the clock, but now we were starting to feel fatigued.

> I was upset with myself, but I knew it would do more damage if I couldn't leave that moment in the past and move on mentally.

Ten minutes to go. A couple of subs came in, and I tried to stay aware of the changes and who would be where, not wanting to make a mistake that might cost us a goal in those last desperate minutes. The seconds crawled by. We kept up our defensive stance, and I have never been so tired or wanted something so badly. Every player was feeling the same, and as we ran out the last few seconds, the only things keeping us going were the nonstop shouts of encouragement from the sidelines. When the whistle *finally* blew, I fell to my knees.

You'd think my first response would have been excitement—screaming, jumping, running to tackle-hug my team—but honestly, I was so physically and mentally exhausted, all I could think was, *Holy cow, that was the longest game I've ever played!* I couldn't even process what that whistle meant except that I got to collapse.

When I finally realized we had just won the World Cup, a crazy flashback sequence started to play in my head. I remembered all the hours of training my team put in, all the extra training *I* did, my first attempt to make the qualifying roster, the phone call from Jill—I relieved it all, but I remember thinking to myself, *Wow, I'm not really that emotional. Shouldn't I be crying right now?*

I didn't really get emotional until I was talking to two of my good friends on the team, Morgan Brian and Syd Leroux. We were chatting about the year we'd had as a team and as individuals and about the journey to get to that moment, and suddenly the reality of where I was and what had just happened hit me. Someone snapped a picture of me, and I look really sad, but that's not how I felt. I'd been holding my breath, waiting for that moment since I first kicked a soccer ball when I was four years old, and now I could finally exhale. It was unreal. I'd never had a lifelong dream come true before, so I didn't know what I was supposed to feel.

BEDLAM!

The immediate aftermath of the game was bedlam, with the crowd screaming, reporters and cameras all over the place, confetti flying through the air, officials trying to corral players, and us players clinging to each other. It was all so surreal, some parts still feel like I might have imagined them, and I don't remember others at all. I do know we did a lap around the field as soon as we could stand, and then everyone went to their families.

All around me, my teammates were finding their families in the stands and hugging them, but I couldn't seem to locate mine. I was really bummed, and as soon as the ceremony onstage was over with, I went back to the family section. I finally found Zach, and I ran to him as

> I'd never had a lifelong dream come true before, so I didn't know what I was supposed to feel.

fast as I could and gave him a big kiss. He let me know our families were going to meet us at the after party that was going to be held for the team later that evening.

Back in the stadium, my team was silly with relief, shock, and joy. We would have been perfectly happy celebrating in the locker room for the rest of the night, but we eventually managed to make it back to the hotel so we could get ready for the party. I don't think I've ever gotten ready so fast in my life—I was going crazy waiting to see my family.

THE CELEBRATION PARTY

When we walked into the party, we were introduced onstage. Suddenly I saw their faces in the crowd, and I didn't hear another word that was said about us. I rushed over and tried to hug everyone at once, and I didn't leave their side the whole night.

> I rushed over and tried to hug everyone at once, and I didn't leave their side the whole night.

Celebrating with my team was great, but I think we were all having the same thoughts and reliving the same memories from a lifetime of chasing this goal. Our families had been there supporting us every step of the way, sharing our victories with us, and so now this victory didn't feel complete without our original "team" close beside us. To be able to celebrate with my family and make them proud was yet another dream come true.

We talked all night, sharing stories about different parts of the game from our perspectives and trading funny stories of things we'd seen that day. Mom told me they'd walked by a group of Outlaws (a U.S. Soccer fan club) from Arizona, and one of them, a man in a blonde wig, had been dressed exactly like me—right down to the blue prewrap headband. My parents had some of those surreal moments as well. My mom said she was of course proud, but there were times during the game when she'd look around at the "We Love Julie" signs and little girls wearing my jersey, and she just kept thinking, *This is the kid I could never get to clean up her room!*

A lot of people stayed at the party until the next morning, but I think I was the first one to leave. I'd played every minute of seven games in the

World Cup tournament, and I needed some sleep.

A DREAM COME TRUE?

The words "a dream come true" get thrown around a lot. Disney princesses, songwriters, and teachers all seem to love that phrase, but what does it actually mean? To dream is to imagine all the possibilities, to think about the future without letting negative voices chime in, and to explore your talents and passions and picture what it might look like if you followed them as far as you could.

Dreaming is great! The phrase "dream come true," though, can be a little deceptive. What I mean by that is that most dreams don't just "come true" on their own. You don't wake up one morning and have everything you dreamed of through the power of positive thinking. A dream is like a compass; it can point the way toward what you want all day long, but you'll never reach it until you follow where your compass is directing you.

My dreams have been pointing the way toward the World Cup for as long as I can remember. With every new team I played for, club I joined, or coach I worked with, those dreams got clearer, stronger, and more focused, but I had to take hundreds of steps in the right direction in order to make them a reality. Dreaming gave me the vision; hard work gave me the skills. Dreaming gave me the goals; my coaches taught me how to get there. You get the idea.

Dreams without action can be

> I'd played every minute of seven games in the World Cup tournament, and I needed some sleep.

> A dream is like a compass; it can point the way toward what you want all day long, but you'll never reach it until you follow where your compass is directing you.

pleasant, but they don't change your life. My dream would never have come true if I'd just waited around for someone to invite me to play in the World Cup. That dream needed determination, a willingness to fail, a willingness to work harder, and the support of my family, friends, and teammates. When you really think about it, dreams don't "come true" as much as they have to be chased down like a soccer ball.

Chasing down my World Cup dream has been a lifelong process. There were times I thought it might get away from me, but as my faith has grown stronger, so has my sense of peace that God will never leave me standing in the middle of the field alone. His picture and purpose for my life are bigger and better than I can imagine, and He'll never leave me without a dream to chase. I'm going to keep playing every minute I can, and as new dreams come along, I'm just going to say, like I did all the way back at the beginning of my career, "Okay, here we go—lead the way!"

Q & A
WITH JULIE

FAVORITES

Q. Favorite movie?
A. There are too many great movies; I can't pick just one!

Q. Favorite fast-food restaurant?
A. Chipotle.

Q. Favorite season?
A. Fall.

Q. Favorite holiday?
A. Christmas.

Q. Favorite holiday tradition?
A. Spending time with family.

Q. Favorite color?
A. Blue.

Q. Favorite healthy food?
A. Avocadoes.

Q. Favorite junk food?
A. Dark chocolate!

Q. Favorite vacation spot?
A. Anywhere that has a beach.

Q. Favorite kind of ice cream?
A. Vanilla bean.

Q. Favorite thing in your closet?
A. Nike shoes.

Q. Favorite emoji?
A. Heart eyes!

Q. Favorite thing to cook?
A. Breads.

Q. Favorite quote?
A. Believe in yourself so strongly that the world can't help but believe in you too.

Q. Favorite Bible verse?
A. Colossians 3:23 and 1 John 4:19.

Q. Favorite game to play with your family (other than soccer)?
A. Pickleball.

DAY IN THE LIFE

Q. Describe your typical pregame ritual.
A. A big breakfast followed by a walk to get coffee, which gives me a chance to move around and start visualizing the game. I talk to my family and FaceTime my husband, and then have

lunch or a pregame meal. I always shower before a game to wake myself up. Then it's pregame prayer with my teammates before finally heading to the game listening to music.

Q. What kind of music pumps you up before a game?
A. My music is all lyrical. I make a playlist for the year of songs I find inspiring or motivating and like the repetition of listening to it all year.

IF

Q. If you could pick any superpower, what would it be?
A. The ability to fly.

Q. If you had more spare time, what hobby would you spend more time on?
A. Learning other languages.

Q. If you could live anywhere, where would it be?
A. Somewhere warm!

Q. If you were an animal, what would you be?
A. A lion.

Q. If you could meet any famous person, whom would it be and why?
A. Lionel Messi; I would love to hear his perspective on the game!

Q. If you could have any kind of pet, what would it be?
A. Two dogs—a big one and a small one.

YOU AND ZACH

Q. Favorite thing to do together?
A. Eat!

Q. Love at first sight or friends first?
A. Love at first sight.

Q. What was your first thought when you met Zach?
A. *That smile. Those eyes!*

Q. What song was your first dance to at your wedding?
A. The acoustic version of "Latch" by Sam Smith.

Q. Who runs faster, you or Zach?
A. Zach.

Q. Last place you traveled together?
A. Turks and Caicos Islands.

Q. How long did you date before getting married?
A. Four years.

Q. Favorite thing about Zach?
A. How he supports me and shows his love.

BEST AND WORST

Q. Least-favorite food?
A. Olives.

Q. What's your most treasured possession? What was it in middle school?
A. Today, it's my wedding ring. In middle school, it was my cleats.

Q. What was the biggest surprise you ever got?
A. My grandma comes up with the most amazing gifts!

Q. Best present you ever got?
A. A cross necklace from Zach.

Q. Most embarrassing moment?
A. Just one?

Q. Biggest fear/phobia?
A. Spiders!

TRAVEL

Q. How many countries have you traveled to?
A. Sixteen.

Q. How many states have you traveled to?
A. Forty.

Q. What's your favorite thing about traveling?
A. Experiencing new things.

Q. What country's food is your favorite?
A. Portugal.

Q. One thing you never travel without?
A. My passport! Or good walking shoes.

Q. What's one place you've never been you'd like to go?
A. Italy.

Q. Where would you most like to return to?
A. England—more live soccer games!

AND A FEW MORE

Q. What's something you've always wanted to try but haven't done yet?
A. Scuba diving.

Q. Have you ever broken any bones?
A. Nope.

Q. What's one thing you wish you knew when you were younger?
A. I wish I'd been further along in my faith at an earlier age.

Q. Would you survive the zombie apocalypse?
A. Yes!

Q. What's your middle name?
A. Beth.

Q. What's a hidden talent of yours?
A. I could probably eat fifteen donuts in one sitting!

Q. What's something you're really bad at?
A. Singing.

Q. What's one thing most people would be surprised to learn about you?
A. I have always wanted to voice a character in an animated movie!